Macbeth

by
William Shakespeare

Literature Guide Developed by Kristen Bowers
for Secondary Solutions®

ISBN-13: 978-0-9845205-9-6

Secondary **Solutions**
The *First* Solution for the Secondary Teacher®
www.4secondarysolutions.com

Macbeth Literature Guide

About This Literature Guide

Secondary Solutions is the endeavor of a high school English teacher who could not seem to find appropriate materials to help her students master the necessary concepts at the secondary level. She grew tired of spending countless hours researching, creating, writing, and revising lesson plans, worksheets, quizzes, tests, and extension activities to motivate and inspire her students, and at the same time, address those ominous content standards. Materials that were available were either juvenile in nature, skimpy in content, or were moderately engaging activities that did not come close to meeting the content standards on which her students were being tested. Frustrated and tired of trying to get by with inappropriate, inane lessons, she finally decided that if the right materials were going to be available to her and other teachers, she was going to have to make them herself. Mrs. Bowers set to work to create one of the most comprehensive and innovative Literature Guide sets on the market. Joined by a middle school teacher with 21 years of secondary school experience, Secondary Solutions began, and has matured into a specialized team of intermediate and secondary teachers who have developed for you a set of materials unsurpassed by all others.

Before the innovation of Secondary Solutions, materials that could be purchased offered a reproducible student workbook and a separate set of teacher materials at an additional cost. Other units provided the teacher with student materials only, and very often, the content standards were ignored. Secondary Solutions provides all of the necessary materials for complete coverage of the literature units of study, including author biographies, pre-reading activities, numerous and varied vocabulary and comprehension activities, study-guide questions, graphic organizers, literary analysis and critical thinking activities, essay and writing ideas, extension activities, quizzes, unit tests, alternative assessment, and much more. Each Guide is designed to address the unique learning styles and comprehension levels of every student in your classroom. All materials are written and presented at the grade level of the learner, and include *extensive coverage of the content standards*. As an added bonus, all teacher materials are included.

As a busy teacher, you don't have time to waste reinventing the wheel. You want to get down to the business of *teaching*. With our professionally developed teacher-written Literature Guides, Secondary Solutions has provided you with the answer to your time management problems, while saving you hours of tedious and exhausting work. Our Guides will allow you to focus on the most important aspects of teaching—the personal, one-on-one, hands-on instruction you enjoy most—the reason you became a teacher in the first place.

The *First* Solution for the Secondary Teacher®
www.4secondarysolutions.com

How to Use Our Literature Guides

Our Literature Guides are based upon the *National Council of the Teachers of English* and the *International Reading Association's* national English/Language Arts Curriculum and Content Area Standards as well as aligned with the National Common Core Standards in English Language Arts in Reading: Literature and Language. The materials we offer allow you to teach the love and full enjoyment of literature, while still addressing the concepts upon which your students are assessed.

These Guides are designed to be used in their sequential entirety, or may be divided into separate parts. *Please do not feel pressure to use everything as is!* We have worked hard to create a variety of helpful materials for you to choose from. Pick and choose materials that fit the needs of *your* students in *your* classroom, in *your* timeframe! The important thing is that the work has been done for you, and you are not forced into extra work.

There are several distinct categories within each Literature Guide:

- ***Exploring Expository Writing***—Worksheets designed to address the exploration and analysis of functional and/or informational materials and of the historical aspects of the text
  - ✓ *Author Biography,* including heritage, beliefs, and customs of the author
  - ✓ *Historical Context,* including allusions and unique diction, comparison of situations across historical eras, analysis of theme relevant to the historical era
  - ✓ *Biographies of relevant non-fictional characters*
- ***Comprehension Check***—Similar to *Exploring Expository Writing,* but designed for comprehension of narrative text—study questions designed to guide students *as they read the text.*
  - ✓ Questions focus on *Reading Comprehension and Analysis* and cover a wide range of questioning based on Bloom's Taxonomy
- ***Standards Focus***—Worksheets and activities that directly address the content standards and allow students extensive practice in literary skills and analysis. *Standards Focus* activities are found within every chapter or section. Some examples:
  - ✓ *Literary Response and Analysis,* including *Figurative Language, Irony, Flashback, Theme, Tone and Mood, Style, and Aesthetic Approach, etc.*
  - ✓ *Writing Strategies,* including developing thesis statements, audience and purpose, sentence combining, concise word choice, developing research questions, etc.
- ***Assessment Preparation***—Vocabulary activities which emulate the types of vocabulary/ grammar proficiency on which students are tested in state and national assessments. *Assessment Preparation* activities are found within every chapter or section. Some examples:
  - ✓ *Writing Conventions,* including *Parts of Speech, Precise Word Choice, Punctuation*
  - ✓ *Vocabulary and Word Development,* including *Context Clues, Connotation/Denotation, Word Roots, Analogies, Literal and Figurative Language*
- ***Quizzes and Tests***—Quizzes are included for each chapter or designated section; final tests as well as alternative assessment are available at the end of each Guide.
- ***Pre-Reading, Post-Reading Activities, Essay/Writing Ideas <u>plus</u> Sample Rubrics***—Each Guide also has its own unique pre-reading, post reading, and essay/writing ideas and alternative assessment activities.

Each Guide contains handouts and activities for varied levels of difficulty. We know that not all students are alike—nor are all teachers. We hope you can effectively utilize every aspect our Literature Guides have to offer—we want to make things easier on you. If you need additional assistance, please email us at info@4secondarysolutions.com. Thank you for choosing Secondary Solutions—The *First* Solution for the Secondary Teacher®.

From the Author of this Literature Guide

To students, and often to teachers themselves, Shakespeare can be as daunting and intimidating as learning a foreign language. Students (and teachers alike) can be overwhelmed by the antiquated diction, unusual syntax, and unfamiliar meter. Teachers can be further overwhelmed with the responsibility of introducing these fundamentals to students—especially when met with hostile, or at the very least, indifferent ears.

One of the pitfalls to trying to teach a required text that you may not be wild about is the fact that most will try to rush through it as fast as possible, to avoid answering questions, or to say you "tried" teaching it, recommending that it be removed from your district's list of required literature. I encourage you to face your fears. With this Guide, you will be able to understand Shakespeare's Macbeth and you will be able to teach your students even the most subtle nuances and seemingly difficult passages.

But how do we as teachers overcome our own intimidation and insecurities (or worse, hatred or fear) of Shakespeare? First, don't try to hide the fact that you, like your students, often feel overwhelmed or intimidated. Start a discussion about it. Let them know that there will be questions they will ask that you may not know the answers to. Encourage them to learn with you. In the beginning, you may honestly have to "fake it 'til you make it." There is nothing wrong with this—and again, this Guide will help you through it.

I applaud you for teaching, for your fortitude, and for purchasing this Guide. By the time you have finished teaching Macbeth, not only will you have a better grasp of the text, but an arsenal you trust with which to teach it. Students may surprise you how much they actually liked the story, and understood it. You may also be surprised by how much you have learned and grown as a teacher.

Good luck to you!

Macbeth
Standards Focus: Elements of Drama

Drama is a form of literature designed to be performed in front of an audience. There are two main types of drama: **comedy** and **tragedy**. Like fiction, dramatic works have a plot, characters, setting, conflict, and one or more themes. It is essential to know the elements of drama when reading a dramatic work.

1. **act**: a division within a play, much like chapters of a novel
2. **aside**: lines that are spoken by a character directly to the audience
3. **cast of characters**: a list of characters presented before the action begins
4. **chorus**: a person or group of people who act as a narrator, commentator, or general audience to the action of the play
5. **comedy**: a humorous work of drama
6. **dialogue**: conversation between two or more characters
7. **drama**: a work of literature designed to be performed in front of an audience
8. **foil**: a character who is nearly opposite of another character; the purpose of a foil (a.k.a. character foil) is to reveal a stark contrast between the two characters, often the protagonist and antagonist
9. **monologue**: a long speech spoken by a character to himself, another character, or to the audience
10. **scene**: a division of an act into smaller parts
11. **soliloquy**: thoughts spoken aloud by a character when he/she is alone, or thinks he/she is alone
12. **stage directions**: italicized comments that identify parts of the setting or the use of props or costumes, give further information about a character, or provide background information; in Shakespeare's plays, stage directions can also appear in brackets, parenthesis, and/or half-brackets
13. **tragedy**: a serious work of drama in which the hero suffers catastrophe or serious misfortune, usually because of his own actions
14. **tragic hero**: a protagonist with a fatal flaw that eventually leads to his demise

Activity: Using the words from the list above, create a 10-question Multiple-Choice quiz. You must use the information/definitions from this page, but you may also add your own knowledge to create your questions. Be sure to create an answer key and keep it on a separate piece of paper. For example:

The two main types of drama are:
    a. plays and monologues   c. histories and biographies
    b. comedies and tragedies   d. monologues and soliloquies

When you have finished, give the "quiz" to a partner and take his or her quiz. Then, check each other's answers, and turn in your quizzes, your answer key, and your scores to your teacher. Your teacher can even find the best questions and use them on a real quiz!

Macbeth

Standards Focus: Literary Elements

Other important elements of drama, especially in Shakespeare's dramatic works, are literary techniques used by the author that make the writing more entertaining and enjoyable. The following is a list of other important elements to know before reading Shakespeare's plays.

- **alliteration**: repetition of consonant sounds at the beginning of words or stressed syllables (i.e. "Peter Piper picked a peck of pickled peppers")

- **allusion**: a literary reference to a well-known work of art, music, history or literature (i.e. "At lovers' perjuries, they say Jove laughs." (Act II, Sc. 2), a reference to Jove [another name for Jupiter, Roman king of the gods])

- **blank verse**: non-rhyming poetry, usually written in iambic pentameter. Most of Shakespeare's plays are written in this form, which is very close to normal speech rhythms and patterns. Often Shakespeare will deviate from this form in order to make a point about the character's state of mind or for other emphasis, like a change in the mood.

- **comic relief**: in a tragedy, a break in the seriousness for a moment of comedy or silliness

- **double entendre**: a word or phrase with more than one meaning, usually when the second meaning is risqué

- **dramatic irony**: when the audience or reader knows something that the characters in the story do not know

- **euphemism**: a substitution of a more pleasant expression for one whose meaning may come across as rude or offensive (i.e. "He passed away," rather than "He died.")

- **figurative language**: writing or speech that is not meant to be taken literally; often used to compare dissimilar objects; figurative language includes metaphor, simile, personification, and hyperbole

- **foreshadowing**: hints of events to occur later in a story

- **iamb**: a unit in poetry consisting of an unstressed syllable followed by a stressed syllable

- **iambic pentameter**: a 10-syllable line divided into 5 iambic feet (one unstressed syllable followed by one stressed syllable). This is the basic rhythm of Shakespeare's verse.

- **imagery**: language that works to evoke images in your mind (i.e. "And with thy bloody and invisible hand / Cancel and tear to pieces that great bond / Which keeps me pale.")

- **irony**: a contradiction between what is expected and what actually is—or appearance versus reality; includes verbal irony, situational irony, and dramatic irony

- **metaphor**: a figure of speech in which a word or phrase is replaced by another, often indicating a likeness or similarity between them (i.e. "Life's but a walking shadow, a poor player...")

- **oxymoron**: when two opposite terms are used together (i.e. "O heavy lightness!")

- **personification**: attributing human characteristics to non-human objects

- **prose**: normal speech rhythm; Shakespeare often wrote certain characters speaking either in all verse or all prose, indicating some personality trait of the character. If the character deviates from his normal form, be aware of a changing state of mind...often prose signals a character slipping into insanity!

- **pun**: a play on words, especially those that sound alike, but have different meanings (i.e. "Ask for me tomorrow and you will find me a grave man")

- **reversal**: the point at which the action of the plot takes an unexpected turn; usually the protagonist learns something about himself and might even regret his decisions, or realizes the affect his decision may have on himself or others

- **rhyming couplet**: two rhyming lines at the end of a speech, signaling that a character is leaving the stage or that the scene is ending

- **simile**: a figure of speech comparing two unlike things that is often introduced by like or as (i.e. "My love is like a red, red rose")

Name _____ Period _____

Macbeth
Pre-Reading Ideas and Activities

Suggested activities **prior to** the study of *Macbeth*:

1. Research the belief in witchcraft and the supernatural in Shakespeare's time. Make a list of Shakespeare's plays that employ the use of witches, ghosts, or other supernatural beings, why Shakespeare used these beings, and the affect it would have had on Shakespeare's audience.

2. Research the monarchy in England and/or Scotland beginning with the reign of James IV, King of Scots. (Note: they intertwine!) Either make a timeline with pictures of the reigning monarchs, or include their names and an interesting fact about each, or both.

3. Create an annotated bibliography of great Shakespeare sites you find on the Internet. You can present your work in PowerPoint or Prezi format, or create your own website, complete with the annotated links, pictures, and more.

4. Create your own scenes in what you believe Shakespeare's language "sounds" like. Some ideas for the scenes: a politician wanting to get to the "top" of the political ladder (maybe a Senator or Congressman, or even President), with his wife pushing him on; a scene in which a woman will do anything to gain the money her parents have in their estate; a scene in which two girls are in love with the same boy, but he only loves one of them, and they have no idea which one. Your teacher will give you guidelines such as number of lines each character must speak, use of props and costumes, etc. Feel free to come up with your own ideas—this can yield great results, so be sure the video camera is ready!

5. Do an Internet search and brochure/report on Elizabethan Era food, dress, social classes, games, weapons, etc. Your teacher will divide the class into small groups and give a topic to share with the rest of the class, or have you work individually on all topics.

6. Conduct further research on Shakespeare and his life. Create a report and/or a timeline of the events of his life.

7. Research theater in Shakespeare's time; famous theaters (The Globe, The Rose), how plays were performed (costumes, location, actors), who saw the plays, how much they cost, what the environment was like, etc.

8. Create a presentation about science, technology, and new inventions of the 16th Century. Include research on: scissors, the spinning wheel, the graphite pencil, the Gregorian Calendar, the musket, the pendulum, the compound microscope, the "water closet," and the thermometer.

9. Create a presentation of famous scientists and inventors of the 16th Century, including: Sir Francis Bacon, Nicolaus Copernicus, Galileo Galilei, Konrad Gessner, Emery Molyneux, Andreas Vesalius, Francis Drake, and Edward Wright.

10. Create a presentation about science, technology, and new inventions of the 17th Century. Include research on: invention of the telescope, steam turbine, barometer, Champagne, the pendulum clock, the first calculator, ice cream, King James Bible, the first submarine, the first dictionary, the discovery of bacteria, among others.

11. Create a presentation of famous scientists and inventors of the 17th Century, including: René Descartes, Thomas Hobbes, Antonie van Leeuwenhoek, John Locke, Isaac Newton, and Blaise Pascal.

12. Create a presentation of famous musicians and composers of the 16th Century, including: Andrea Amati, Giovanni Bassano, William Brade, John Bull, Alfonso Fontanelli, and Hans Leo Hassler.

13. Create a presentation of famous musicians and composers of the 17th Century, including: Johann Sebastian Bach, Georg Friedrich Handel, Claudio Monteverdi, Johann Pachelbel, and Antonio Vivaldi.

14. Create a presentation about the role/life of women of the 16th and 17th Centuries, including limits and restrictions, family and child-rearing, church, and social obligations and expectations.

15. Create a presentation of famous leaders and significant people of the 16th Century, including: Henry VII of England, Martin Luther, Henry VIII of England, King Francis I of France, Suleiman the Magnificent, Charles V, Michel Nostradamus, John Calvin, Mary I of England, John Knox, and Leonardo da Vinci.

16. Create a presentation of famous leaders of the 17th Century, including: Charles I and Charles II of England, Queen Elizabeth, James I of England, Leopold I, Louis XIV of France, Peter the Great, Queen Anne of Austria.

17. Create a presentation of famous writers and poets of the 16th Century, including: Miguel de Cervantes, John Donne, Thomas Heywood, Ben Jonson, Thomas Kyd, Christopher Marlowe, Miyamoto Musashi, Pierre de Ronsard, and Edmund Spenser.

18. Create a presentation of Shakespeare's contemporaries, including: Miguel de Cervantes, Daniel Defoe, John Donne, John Dryden, John Milton, Moliere, Samuel Pepys, Jean Racine, and Félix Lope de Vega.

19. Help your teacher put together a bulletin board of a culmination of these research projects and findings to have on display in your classroom. Have a contest among your classes for the best bulletin board display. This also looks great for Back to School Night or Open House—and administrators love it! Make your teacher proud!

20. Create a bulletin board of Shakespeare's sonnets, and/or plays, pictures of characters (can be movie posters), and anything else you can think of. Have a contest among your classes for the best bulletin board display.

Name _____ Period _____

Macbeth
Anticipation Guide Pre-Reading Activity

Directions*: The following statements are designed to get you thinking before we delve into the text of Macbeth. Answer each question writing "YES" if you agree with the statement, "NO" if you disagree, or "Not Sure" if you are not convinced either way about a statement. For each, explain/justify in one or two sentences why you chose your answer, including examples or reasoning. Be prepared to discuss and justify your responses in class.*

_____ 1.   *Too much ambition can be dangerous.*

Justification: _____

_____

_____ 2.   *We cannot control our fate.*

Justification: _____

_____

_____ 3.   *It is not always easy to resist temptation.*

Justification: _____

_____

_____ 4.   *It is not fate, but our own human will, that controls us.*

Justification: _____

_____

_____ 5.   *We all have the power to control our own destiny.*

Justification: _____

_____

_____ 6.   *Violence leads to more violence.*

Justification: _____

_____

_____ 7.   *Everyone battles good and evil within themselves.*

Justification: _____

_____

_____ 8.   *No matter who we are, our conscience will eventually help us decide right*
from wrong.

Justification: _____

_____

_____ 9.   *I always listen to my conscience.*

Justification: _____

_____

_____ 10. *Most people will do whatever they need to do to reach a goal.*

Justification: _____

_____

_____ 11. *We should be careful who we trust.*

Justification: _____

_____

_____ 12. *There are people in this world who have the ability to predict the future.*

Justification: _____

_____

_____ 13. *It is wrong to give in to temptation.*

Justification: _____

_____

_____ 14. *It is impossible to make someone do something they don't want to do.*

Justification: _____

_____

_____ 15. *No matter what people have, they always want even more.*

Justification: _____

_____

_____ 16. *Husbands and wives always should support each other in their goals and aspirations.*

Justification: _____

_____

_____ 17. *There is never a good reason to kill another person.*

Justification: _____

_____

_____ 18. *I believe we should wait for someone or something to guide us through our lives, rather than making things happen on our own.*

Justification: _____

_____

Macbeth
Informational Text: Author Biography
William Shakespeare

William Shakespeare is widely believed to have been the greatest playwright in history. His plays are continually produced and students around the world read his works in school. Shakespeare is known for his ability to depict the depth of human character and for his skill in illustrating issues to which, for hundreds of years, people around the world can relate.

Shakespeare's father, John Shakespeare, was a wealthy business owner and active citizen of Stratford-upon-Avon in England. He married Shakespeare's mother, Mary Arden, in 1557, and William was born on April 23, 1564.

During the sixteenth century, waves of the Black Plague ravaged England and William was lucky to have survived. Two of his sisters, Joan and Margaret, died from the affliction. William's younger brother, Gilbert, fortunately escaped the deadly epidemic and had a long and successful career as a tradesman. Later, John and Mary Shakespeare had four more children: Joan (named after their firstborn), Anne (who died at age eight), Richard, and Edmund, who eventually followed in William's footsteps as an actor.

Shakespeare began his education at the age of six or seven at the Stratford grammar school, known as the King's New School of Stratford-upon-Avon. His lessons were primarily in Latin, but William also likely learned in English. Shakespeare was taken out of school at about the age of thirteen, due to his father's financial problems at this time. It is believed that William continued his studies on his own, however, educating himself as much as possible. The events of William's life between the age of thirteen and when he emerged in London as an actor, is generally unknown. However, it is recorded that in 1582, at the age of eighteen he married Anne Hathaway, who was eight years older than him and pregnant at the time.

Shakespeare's first child, Susanna, was born in 1583. In 1585, twins Hamnet and Judith were born. In 1596, Hamnet died of unknown causes. The loss was said to have affected William deeply. Shakespeare's grief and loss is said to be expressed in his writing.

Little is known about Shakespeare's life during the years of 1585 to 1592, before he appeared as an actor in London. It is believed he spent this time perfecting his craft as an actor and playwright. By 1592, Shakespeare was already an established and respected actor in London. Productions of Henry IV and The Comedy of Errors were performed by Pembroke's Men, a popular acting troupe who often performed for

Queen Elizabeth. In 1594, Shakespeare joined another acting troupe, Lord Chamberlain's Men, and it was while he was with this group that Shakespeare wrote Romeo and Juliet, Richard II, King John, and others.

Although Shakespeare was never wealthy, he lived a comfortable life, buying a home in Stratford in 1597. He became part-owner of the most popular theater in London, the Globe Theater, in 1599, and the Blackfriars Theater in 1603. Shakespeare continued to act until 1613, when he returned to Stratford to retire. Shakespeare is believed to have died on April 23, 1616, exactly 52 years to the day of his birth.

Comprehension Check: Author Biography

Directions*: Answer the following questions using complete sentences on a separate piece of paper.*

1. When and where was William Shakespeare born?

2. Write an original thesis statement that best summarizes the article.

3. How old was Shakespeare when he married Anne Hathaway? Why might his marriage be considered controversial?

4. Rewrite the following paragraph to improve cohesion and logic:
   Shakespeare's first child, Susanna, was born in 1583. In 1585, twins Hamnet and Judith were born. In 1596, Hamnet died of unknown causes. The loss was said to have affected William deeply. Shakespeare's grief and loss is said to be expressed in his writing.

5. Besides writing plays, what else did Shakespeare do in London?

6. What is significant about the date of Shakespeare's death?

7. Does this article primarily contain *facts* or *opinions*? How do you know?

8. How is the information in this article arranged: problem/solution, cause/effect, compare/contrast, or chronological? How can you tell?

9. If you were given an assignment to find out more information about the life of William Shakespeare, what 3 questions would you like to find answers for in your research?

10. Some critics believe that author biographies are sometimes helpful in understanding what a person wrote. Many other critics, however, feel that an author's life should not be brought into the analysis of a piece of literature. In other words, they feel we do not need to know about Shakespeare in order to understand or appreciate *Macbeth* or any of his other works. Do you feel it is important to know an author's life history in order to understand his work? Explain your response.

Macbeth
Working with Shakespeare's Language

When Shakespeare wrote his sonnets and plays, the language he used was popular and would have been easily recognized by 17th century audiences. However, today we have a more difficult time comprehending the words Shakespeare used. What we must remember is that Shakespeare's words can be easily "translated" into modern English, and once we become familiar with these words, it becomes easier to read and understand the language. It is then that we are able to appreciate the story Shakespeare is trying to tell.

On the next page is a list of common words and phrases found in Shakespeare's works, along with a modern translation of the words or phrases.

Directions: *Working with a partner, choose from the following three scenarios to write a scene between two people using modern-day English. Each character must have at least 10 lines (at least 3 words per line). Next, using the words on the next page, "translate" your scene into the Old English language that Shakespeare would have used.*

Scenario #1: Write a scene in which two girls (or boys) have a crush on the same boy (or girl), but don't know it. In the scene, either have the girls (boys) discover their problem, or have them talk about the same boy (girl) and never figure it out.

Scenario #2: Write a scene in which a teenager wants to go out with someone her parents don't like. Have the teen explain why he/she should be allowed to go out with this person, and have the parents explain their point of view.

Scenario #3: Write a scene in which a girl (or boy) persuades her boyfriend (or girlfriend) to do something they shouldn't do—whether it is illegal or immoral. Either have the boyfriend (or girlfriend) agree or oppose the idea.

Once you have written your 20+ line scenes in Shakespeare's language, present your scene in front of the class training your eyes and ears to the beauty of the language and enjoying an exercise in public speaking and performance!

Working with Shakespeare's Language

'tis: it is
'twere: it were
'twill: it will
adieu: expression meaning "good bye"
an: if
anon: at once; soon
art: are
attend: listen; pay attention
ay: yes
bade: asked; requested
beseech: beg
bid: to wish; ask
camest: came
canst: can
desirest: desire; want
discourses: speaks
dost: do
doth: does
farewell: good-bye
fellow: a young man
flirt-girls: flirtacious young women
foe: enemy
God gi god-den: "good day" or "good evening"
good morrow: "good morning"
hark ye: listen
heavy: sad
hie: go
hist: a sound to get someone's attention, like "hey"
hither: here
kinsmen: family member; relative

lord: an expression of respect towards a man
maid: an unmarried young girl
mark: listen; pay attention to
merrily: happily
methinks: I think
mine: my
morn: morning
morrow: tomorrow
naught: nothing
nay: no
pray: ask; plead with
quoth: said
repliest: reply
sirrah: fellow; young man
skains-mates: mischievous companions
spake: spoke
thee: you
thine: mine
thither: there
thou: you (informal)
thy: your or my
went'st: went
wert: were
whither: where
will: desire
wilt: will
woe: grief
woo: to court; date; flirt
wot: know
would: wish
wouldst: would
yea: yes

Name _____ Period _____

Macbeth
Appreciating Shakespeare's Language

Shakespeare's work was meant to be seen and heard as a performance; it was not necessarily intended to be read. Therein lies the first problem to reading Shakespeare in a classroom. Shakespeare used an extensive array of vocabulary, including archaic language, an unfamiliar grammatical structure, and a "backward" arrangement of words in his sonnets and plays. The combination of these elements can make reading Shakespeare difficult for most people. The trick to reading Shakespeare's works is to try to get the idea or "gist" of what the characters are saying, rather than trying to figure out what every single word means.

Early Modern English: While Shakespeare did speak an earlier form of English than we currently do, it was still considered modern English—which should make reading his work less intimidating than reading Chaucer, for example, who spoke an even earlier form of English. Shakespeare used a few words and conventions that have disappeared, such as *hath* instead of *has* and *doth* instead of *does*. In fact, these words were disappearing from use in his time and he used them mainly for dramatic and linguistic affect. The same is true for *thee, thou,* and *thy*, which were rarely used in his time, but Shakespeare felt those words were appropriate to convey certain messages in his works.

With this in mind, try to pay attention to when and why Shakespeare seems to choose to use language that is slightly archaic: he may have a reason for it. For instance, *thee, thou,* and *thy*, are more formal forms of the pronoun *you* (just like *usted*, in Spanish, is a formal form of *tu*); sometimes in Shakespeare's language, a shift from *you* to *thou*—or the other way around—is a signal to the audience.

According to the *The Cambridge Encyclopedia of the English Language*, ed. David Crystal (CUP: 1995), pg. 71:

> During **Early Modern English**, [the language of Shakespeare's time] the distinction between subject and object uses of *ye* and *you* gradually disappeared, and *you* became the norm in all grammatical functions and social situations. *Ye* continued in use, but by the end of the 16th century it was restricted to archaic, religious, or literary contexts. By 1700, the *thou* forms were also largely restricted in this way.
>
> By the time of Shakespeare, *you* had developed the number ambiguity it retains today, being used for either singular or plural; but in the singular it also had a role as an alternative to *thou / thee*. It was used by people of lower rank or status to those above them (such as ordinary people to nobles, children to parents, servants to masters, nobles to the monarch), and was also the standard way for the upper classes to talk to each other. By contrast, *thou / thee* were used by people of higher rank to those beneath them, and by the lower classes to each other; also, in elevated poetic style, in addressing God, and in talking to witches, ghosts, and other supernatural beings. There were also some special cases: for example, a husband might address his wife as *thou*, and she reply with *you*.

Of particular interest are those cases where an extra emotional element entered the situation, and the use of *thou* or *you* broke the expected conventions. *Thou* commonly expressed special intimacy or affection; *you*, formality, politeness, and distance. *Thou* could also be used, even by an inferior to a superior, to express such feelings as anger and contempt.

Shakespeare's Vocabulary: Another point of frustration for Shakespeare's reader is his choice of words. Remember that Shakespeare was an artist and his words were his tools; if he spoke the way everyone spoke, or used the same words in the same way that everyone else did, his art would not be distinctive and we would probably not read still read his works today. Also, keep in mind that Shakespeare had a vocabulary of about 29,000 words: almost twice that of an American college student today. More importantly, words such as *dwindle* and *assassination* are actually Shakespeare's invention and had never been used before him.

Words, Words, Words: Not only did Shakespeare use new words, he liked to use them in clever ways and often in a strange order. Think about how Yoda speaks in the *Star Wars* movies. We understand exactly what he says, even though the word order sounds mixed up to our ears. This is exactly what Shakespeare does at times, which can make reading Shakespeare difficult.

By reading and "translating" the following lines into modern English, see if you can figure out what Shakespeare meant. Remember that Shakespeare often rearranged wording or left out words in a sentence to make the rhythm fit iambic pentameter.

"Dismayed not this our captains, Macbeth and Banquo?"
"Went it not so?"
"Is not thy master with them?"
"To me you speak not."
"Know you not he has?"
"Retire we to our chamber."

Verse and Prose: Though Shakespeare sometimes writes in *prose* (ordinary speech), he is most famous for his *verse*, or poetry. The most common form of verse he used was *iambic pentameter*, which means each line contains five *iambs*, or a total of ten syllables. An iamb is a unit of verse consisting of an *unstressed* syllable followed by a *stressed* syllable. Shakespeare also uses rhymes (end rhymes) both at the end of lines and within them (internal rhyme). Sometimes Shakespeare employs blank verse, which is unrhymed poetry, usually in iambic pentameter.

Macbeth

Informational Text: Theater in Shakespeare's Time

Shakespeare is often misunderstood or underappreciated by the modern reader. Many have suggested that this is due to the popular approach to his works; that is, reading them as merely a text when they are, in actuality, much more. Shakespeare wrote for the theater—his theater—with the intent that his work would reach the stage. Thus, when his works are read as one might read a story, many feel that there are gaps in the story, as indeed there are. Under the circumstances, Shakespeare intended these gaps to be filled by the action on the stage. Difficult conversations would be made more coherent through the gestures and facial expressions of the actors. Even the audience would contribute to the story

17th Century drawing of the Globe Theater

through their reactions. Drama is meant to be ephemeral, not static, so trying to force a dramatic work to be read like a book may result in frustration. To help you understand what you read, it is important that you understand some aspects of the theater in Shakespeare's time.

Much has changed since Shakespeare lived over five hundred years ago, and the theater is no exception. If a person from the present time were to walk into a theater in London during the 16th century, he would be met with a very different sight than what he is used to. A stage in the 1500s consisted of a platform that rose about five feet from the ground, much like the theaters of today. One would notice, however, that unlike the auditorium seating we have come to expect, the seating arrangement consisted of space along three sides of the stage where spectators might stand, and three stories, each with its own gallery, where others might sit. The people who stood closest to the stage, called *groundlings*, were often a rowdy and difficult group who would have paid a mere penny to see the show. The people who sat in seats along the balconies of each story would have paid a penny more, and were generally the more educated, better behaved, upper-class citizens.

The Globe, where many of Shakespeare's plays were staged, is believed to have been very large and elegant, with pillars, arches, and other impressive architectural features. It has been computed that an average-sized theater of the time might have held anywhere from 2,000 to 3,000 spectators—huge compared to many community and professional theaters of today.

Behind the stage was the tiring house that served as a versatile backdrop for the shows and where the actors would prepare for the performance. Most scenes would have been staged downstage (closer to the audience) as there was no way to amplify the actors' voices at that time. If, however, a scene required a discovery of some kind, a curtain upstage (farthest from the audience) would be used to reveal an actor. There were also doors to the left and right of the stage where actors entered and exited, in addition to trap doors in the floor. Plays were performed during the day, as artificial lighting would have been limited to torches or candles. No scenery was used, so the audience was often forced to use their imagination. Often, a character's speech told where and when a scene took place. Props, which were used in abundance, also aided in establishing setting.

Actors of the time would have been like today's celebrities—dressed in the best styles of the day. Many were rumored to be vagabonds and vagrants—stories which were often embellished to make the actors sound more interesting. Specific actors were known for playing very specific roles, such as the king, or the clown, or the lover, and often plays were written with a certain actor in mind. Women were not allowed to perform publicly, so all female roles would have been played by men.

Plays were written under general categories: *tragedy*, which ends sadly and often with the demise of the main character; *comedy*, which ends happily, usually with a wedding or other celebration; *history*, which dramatizes a fictional historical event; *romance*, which is a more serious form of comedy with strange, fantastic, or supernatural elements. Most importantly, it is crucial to keep in mind that the meanings of the words tragedy, comedy, history, and romance in the dramatic sense are not the same as the meanings we commonly associate them with today. Tragedy, though serious in its nature, does not necessarily mean that every aspect of the play will be serious. Comedy, though it often includes humor, does not mean that every scene will be light-hearted and laughable, and in fact, most of Shakespeare's comedies end with—of all things—a wedding.

Name _____ Period _____

Comprehension Check: Shakespeare's Theater

Directions: *Based upon the article* Shakespeare's Theater, *answer the following questions on a separate piece of paper using complete sentences.*

1. Why do some readers find Shakespeare's writing difficult to understand? Explain. How do you feel about Shakespeare's language? Why?

2. What would you suggest that a reader do to better prepare himself for Shakespeare's writing to make it more understandable, and therefore, more enjoyable?

3. What does the word *ephemeral* mean in paragraph one? Why might this quality of drama make a play more difficult to read than a novel would be?

4. What kind of people would you expect to see in a theater (one in which live drama is performed) today? Are the people you imagine different from the people Shakespeare would have expected? How?

5. What are some conveniences that theaters have today that someone in Shakespeare's time could probably never imagine?

6. How are today's actors or celebrities similar to the actors of Shakespeare's time? How are they different?

7. Briefly explain the four types of drama. How are these types of drama different from what we might expect?

Macbeth

Informational Text: Witches, Superstition, and Ghosts

In Shakespeare's time, many people deeply believed in the power and influence of superstition, the power of magic, and in "other-worldly" creatures, such as ghosts and witches. When strange or unexplainable things would happen in the Elizabethan era, many attributed these happenings to the influence of the supernatural, whereas today, we would likely be able to explain things scientifically. Audiences would have been easily led to believe that a character saw a ghost in front of him, or that he would listen to witches' predictions, as in *Macbeth*.

Witches

People from all walks of life and income levels looked to the supernatural to explain the unexplainable. In 1591, it was believed that a group of witches attempted to murder King James I of Scotland, which led to his study of the occult, and ultimately his book on the persecution and punishment of witches, *Daemonologie*, published in 1597.

Many of these superstitions and beliefs stemmed from Celtic and Viking pagan beliefs and traditions that existed thousands of years before. "White" witches and apothecaries who doled out homemade remedies, including potions and chants to heal the sick, were seen as healers, and were welcome throughout the community. By the Elizabethan era, this distinction was gone, and those who had any sort of unexplainable power were considered evil and a harmful and mischievous threat to society. People blamed witches for the Black plague, bad crops, deaths, illnesses, and fires. Those who were accused of practicing witchcraft were usually old, poor, unmarried outcasts of society, but for a period of time, fear and paranoia running rampant, accusations of witchcraft led to the torture and death of hundreds of innocent women and several men.

Superstition

Those in Shakespeare's time also wholeheartedly believed in superstition. It was believed to be bad luck if they walked under a ladder. According to beliefs of the time, the ladder leaning against a wall was representative of the Holy Trinity. Walking under the ladder was considered breaking the Trinity, and tantamount to blaspheming God. Another strong superstition involved sneezing. If a person opened their mouth to sneeze, this was considered an entry point by which the devil could enter one's body. Saying "God bless you" protected the sneezing person from the devil's breach. Elizabethans also believed that if you stirred a pot counter-clockwise, the contents of the pot would be poisoned, and could bring bad luck to everyone who ate the food.

Bad luck could also be brought upon a person by possessing a peacock feather, crossing the path of a black cat, spilling salt, or leaving a door open. Conversely, touching the hand of a prisoner who was about to be hanged, a cow's breath, or spitting into a fire could bring good luck—as could iron, silver, fire, salt, and running water.

Ghosts

The Elizabethans witnessed a time of great strife throughout Europe. They were still reeling from the fight between the Catholics and the Protestants that bloodied the monarchy and led to the execution of hundreds. They saw Queen Elizabeth I's own mother, Anne Boleyn beheaded by her own husband, when Elizabeth was two years old. And later, they saw Elizabeth herself imprison and execute Mary, Queen of Scots in 1587.

The Catholics believed that there was a place called Purgatory, which was a sort of "holding cell" for those who had died, before they were placed in heaven or hell. Ghosts were merely those in Purgatory, waiting to be cleansed of all sin before their placement. Some believe that ghosts were put on earth to serve out their time in Purgatory before they were "moved on."

The Protestants, however, did not believe in a place called Purgatory, but rather, that souls were immediately sent to heaven or hell. Two beliefs existed: First, it was believed that the bodies of the dead were inhabited by spirits and that these spirits came back to cause havoc. Secondly, it was also believed that ghosts were a figment of the mind—that they were simply a hallucination or an illusion.

One of the most influential works of literature of the Elizabethan era that stirred the question of the existence of ghosts was Shakespeare's very own *Hamlet*. While it is not clear whether Shakespeare himself truly believed in ghosts or spirits, he certainly enjoyed fascinating and horrifying his audiences with the ghost of Hamlet's father in his wildly popular play.

Name _____ Period _____

Macbeth
Informational Text: The Real Story

It is interesting to note that Shakespeare's play *Macbeth* was based loosely on true stories about real people. In fact, it is believed that Shakespeare wrote the play for King James I and VI, who was king of both England and Scotland at the time. Allegedly using the *Chronicles of England, Scotland, and Ireland* (1587) by Raphael Holinshed as his source of information, Shakespeare set out to create a realistic fictional drama based on a true story.

The real King Duncan I (Donnchad mac Crínáin), nicknamed "the sick" was the King of Scotland (called Alba) from 1034 to 1040. He was the grandson of Malcolm II, who was killed in battle in 1034. Duncan had two sons, Malcolm III, and Donald III. According to records, Duncan was young and weak and was seen as a terrible and ineffective leader. His ascension to the throne at age 17 caused turmoil in the family, as the kingship was to have alternated between the two branches of the royal line. Many believed his cousin, Macbeth (Mac Bethad mac Findlaích), should have had claim to the throne through his mother. This caused strife in the family, which would continue for hundreds of years.

After Duncan was killed in battle by Macbeth in 1040, Macbeth took the throne and became King of Scotland. Macbeth reigned successfully for 17 years, and he was said to be a powerful and strong leader. However, Duncan's son Malcolm wanted revenge against Macbeth, and felt that he should have inherited the throne after his father's death. In 1054, Malcolm III joined forces with Earl Siward to defeat him at the battle of Dunsinnan. It was not until 1057 that Macbeth was completely overthrown and Malcolm III took the throne as King of Scotland.

Malcolm III Canmore reigned from 1058 to 1093.

Macbeth

Informational Text: Gunpowder Plot of 1605

The Monarchy

The Gunpowder Plot of 1605 was an attempt by a group of Catholics led by Robert Catesby and Guy Fawkes to overthrow and assassinate King James I of England and VI of Scotland.

For decades, the battle between Catholics and Protestants in England was one of the bloodiest times in English history. In 1533, King Henry VIII took control of the English Church from Rome. This quickly caused problems, as the English people now had to swear allegiance to the newly formed Protestant Church of England, led by the King as the Supreme Head of the Church of England in 1534. Over time, he strove to take all power away from the Catholic Church, and even declared his marriage to Catholic Catherine of Aragon invalid after the Catholic Church refused to grant him a divorce. They had a daughter, Mary.

After Henry VIII divorced, he married longtime mistress Anne Boleyn, with whom he had a daughter, Elizabeth, who would eventually become Queen of England. After Anne Boleyn failed to give him a son, Henry had her arrested for high treason, and she was beheaded a month later, in May of 1536.

Although Henry's son Edward VI inherited the throne after Henry's death, many believed the throne still should rightfully belong to Henry's daughter Mary. After Edward VI died at age 15, Mary fought for and gained the throne, becoming Queen of England and Scotland—declaring her kingdom Catholic once again. She earned the title "Bloody Mary" after executing hundreds of Protestants. After Mary failed to have any children, it was declared that Elizabeth would take over the throne in the case of Mary's death. In November 1558, Mary died and Elizabeth took over as Queen of England.

Not surprisingly, Elizabeth established the English Protestant Church, which has evolved into the modern Church of England. Despite numerous courtships, Elizabeth never married and never had children, leaving in question who would become her successor. Many Catholics believed her cousin Mary, Queen of Scots should succeed, however Elizabeth saw Mary as her adversary and a threat. Elizabeth quickly imprisoned her (where she remained for 19 years) and later executed her for treason in 1587.

In the months before Elizabeth died, the English Secretary of State Robert Cecil negotiated with Mary's son James VI of Scotland to take the English throne. The Catholics, however, sought to transfer the throne to Lady Arbella Stuart, Elizabeth's cousin. Instead, in March 1603, James I (who was also King James VI of Scotland at the time) became King of England and Ireland.

The Gunpowder Plot of 1605

Although James was Protestant, he was viewed as more sympathetic of the Catholic faith than his predecessors. However, after his wife, Queen Anne was secretly sent a rosary— Catholic prayer beads—James was incensed and denounced the Catholic Church. He began to exorbitantly fine those who did not attend the Protestant church, and eventually a bill was introduced that threatened to banish or persecute all followers of the Catholic Church. He also ordered all Catholic priests to leave England.

Before the Gunpowder Plot, several other attempts to rid England of King James were made. In what became known as the Bye Plot, two priests conspired to kidnap and hold the king in the Tower of London until he agreed to be more tolerant of Catholics. The Main Plot, an attempt to remove James and replace him with Arbella Stuart, was also hatched at about the same time. Both plots were thwarted and all those involved were arrested. The two priests were later executed.

The Gunpowder Plot was an attempt to kill King James and several other important targets, and to kidnap James's daughter, Princess Elizabeth, whom the conspirators aimed to place on the throne. Believed to be the main conspirator was Robert Catesby, who concocted the plan and rallied the group in 1604.

The plan was to rent a house near the House of Parliament, fill it with gunpowder, and then blow it up with King James and others inside it. After a serious of changes of plans, by March 1605, the men had filled a space under the House of Lords full of 36 barrels of gunpowder. As they gained followers and fellow conspirators, their circle of trust was breached, and the idea began to slip into the ears of others. After attempting to anonymously warn Catholic members of the Parliament to avoid going to work that day, suspicions grew. A search party was sent out and it was then that the royal court discovered the gunpowder and Guy Fawkes, who was eventually tortured to give the names of the other conspirators. The conspirators were tried and hanged in 1606.

November 5th is now Guy Fawkes Night, a night of festival in Great Britain and other British colonies. Fireworks are set off, bonfires are set and "guys" (dummies made of cotton or hay to represent either Fawkes or the Pope) are burned on the bonfires. British children make the "guy" in advance, then walk the street asking for money for the "guy," which children often use for fireworks.

Name _____ Period _____

Macbeth
Historical Context: Map of 11th Century Scotland

Name _____ Period _____

Macbeth
Shakespeare's Style
The Sonnet Form and Iambic Pentameter

Shakespeare wrote 154 sonnets in addition to his plays. In fact, he even added sonnets into his plays. Most of his sonnets were related to the topic of love, and were often written in a sequel-like fashion. Before we dive into reading an entire play, we will be approaching Shakespeare's style in a smaller poem, called a sonnet. The word sonnet comes from the Italian word sonnetto, meaning "little song."

The Shakespearean sonnet almost always follows the same format. It has 14 lines with approximately 10 syllables each line. Each line of the sonnet is written in iambic pentameter. The prefix pent means "five." A line of iambic pentameter consists of 10 syllables, or five iambs of two syllables each. An iamb is an "unstressed" syllable followed by a "stressed" syllable. When written, the "U" symbols mean unstressed, and the "/" indicates a stressed syllable.

To understand the idea of a stressed or an unstressed syllable, think about the syllables of some common names. The name Christopher can be divided into three syllables: Chris/to/pher. If we place the stress, or the emphasis, on the "Chris" it would look like this:

/   U   U
Chris / to / pher

If we place the emphasis on the "to" the name would sound odd to our ears, and look like this:

U   /   U
Chris / to / pher

When analyzing a line of Shakespeare's work, it would look like this:

U /	U /	U /	U /	U /
Let me	not to	the mar	riage of	true minds	(from Sonnet 116)

Finally, Shakespearean sonnets always follow the same rhyme scheme: ABABCDCDEFEFGG, ending with the rhyming couplet, or two rhyming lines.

Now that the technical terms have been introduced, it is time to put that knowledge to work in a practical activity.

Directions: *Read the sonnet on the next page. This sonnet is one of the most famous of Shakespeare's sonnets: Sonnet 23. Read and analyze this sonnet, paying careful attention to the rhyme scheme and the pattern of syllables. Then, using the chart, divide the sonnet into syllables and label its rhyme scheme. Finally, label the stressed and unstressed syllables using the / and U symbols. The first line has been done for you.*

Shakespeare's Style
The Sonnet Form and Iambic Pentameter

1 As an unperfect actor on the stage,
2 Who with his fear is put beside his part,
3 Or some fierce thing replete with too much rage,
4 Whose strength's abundance weakens his own heart;
5 So I, for fear of trust, forget to say
6 The perfect ceremony of love's rite,
7 And in mine own love's strength seem to decay,
8 O'ercharg'd with burthen of mine own love's might.
9 O! let my looks be then the eloquence
10 And dumb presagers of my speaking breast,
11 Who plead for love, and look for recompense,
12 More than that tongue that more hath more express'd.
13 O! learn to read what silent love hath writ:
14 To hear with eyes belongs to love's fine wit.

1	2	3	4	5	6	7	8	9	10	Rhyme Scheme
U As	/ an	U un	/ per	U fect	/ ac	U tor	/ on	U the	/ stage	A
									part	B
									rage	A

Macbeth
Shakespeare's Style
Sonnet Quiz

Directions: *Write "**true**" or "**false**" on the line before the "True or False?" questions. Write the **letter** of the best response to the multiple choice questions on the line provided.*

1. _____ True or False? Shakespeare wrote about 60 sonnets.

2. _____ A Shakespearean sonnet has how many lines?
   a. 10
   b. 14
   c. 12
   d. 16

3. _____ True or False? An iamb consists of one unstressed and one stressed syllable.

4. _____ The last two lines of a Shakespearean sonnet are called:
   a. iambic pentameter
   b. unstressed pair
   c. rhyming couplet
   d. stressed doublet

5. _____ True or False?   Pentameter means that a line is written in 2 iambs.

6. _____ A line in a Shakespearean sonnet has approximately:
   a. 8 syllables
   b. 10 syllables
   c. 12 syllables
   d. 14 syllables

7. _____ True or False? Shakespearean sonnets always follow the same rhyme scheme.

8. _____ True or False? The word sonnet comes from a word meaning "little song."

9. (Worth 2 points) Using the stressed and unstressed syllables, scan the following line:

   Two   households   both   alike   in   dignity

Macbeth
Journal Ideas/Discussion Topics

The following Journal Ideas/Discussion Topics are suggested activities to be used during or after the study of *Macbeth*. These journal topics can be used to facilitate discussion during reading, as a personal journal/reading log, or as essay/writing prompts before, during, or after reading *Macbeth*. Suggestions on when to give prompts have been provided.

*After reading the **Author Biography** (pgs. 10-12):*

> Discuss/journal what you know about Shakespeare and his time, including any possible fears and apprehension you may have towards Shakespeare and his works, what you know about the way Shakespeare's plays are written, and/or why his writing is so popular.

*During/after reading **Act One**:*

- Journal the typical characteristics of both good and bad leaders. Are leaders born or are they made? List the attributes of your ideal "leader"— how he/she would act, reason, negotiate, follow, etc. Can this leadership be used for evil deeds? How?

- Are people born good or born evil? Can they change? Do they? Or do each of us have a battle of good and evil within us? What might push us over the edge either way?

- What are your personal beliefs about fate or destiny? Do you believe your life is mapped out for you, or do you believe that you decide your life's path? What about "other" interventions—such as God or the power of suggestion? Explore your feelings and beliefs in the ideas of fate versus free will.

*During/after reading **Act Two**:*

- Discuss/journal a time when you wanted something so badly you would do almost anything to get it. What was it? When? What was the result? If you were able to get what you wanted, how did it feel? If you weren't, how did that feel? Have you ever gone too far to get what you wanted? How did that feel? Have you heard the line, "Be careful what you wish for; you may just get it." What do you think it means?

- Discuss/journal a time you have done something you deeply regret doing. What made you want to do it in the first place? Were you coerced in any way? Did you ignore your conscience, or did it even occur to you that you might regret your decision? Will the decision have deep or just superficial repercussions? If you had the chance to do it all over again, what would you have done differently?

- Is there someone in your life who is a big influence on you, either in a good or a bad way? What personality characteristics make this person so influential? Why do you think you listen to this person? Do you ever "stand up" to this person? Why or why not? Has this person ever influenced you to do something really great or something really bad? Explain.

*During/after reading **Act Three**:*

- Many people believe we all have an "inner voice" or instinct telling us something. Sometimes, we consciously ignore our inner voice and do something we probably should not have done. Sometimes we listen to our inner voice, and it has gotten us out of trouble or kept us from a dangerous situation. Discuss a time when you ignored or followed your inner voice.

- Everyone has felt jealous at one time or another in his or her life. Discuss a time when you were jealous of someone else. Why were you jealous? How did you feel towards the other person? How did you feel towards yourself? Were you jealous of the person, or were you jealous that he or she had something you really wanted? How did you deal with your jealousy?

- We have all heard some variation of "I told you so!" at one time in our lives. Journal/discuss a time when someone tried to warn, caution, or advise you and you didn't listen to them. What happened? What was the outcome? Would you do things differently or the same in the future, knowing what you know now?

*During/after reading **Act Four***:

- Do you believe in ghosts or other supernatural creatures such as aliens, vampires, the Boogeyman, witches, fairies, etc.? Why or why not? Have you had any experience with what you believed was the supernatural? Why might people believe in other-worldly creatures and beings? Why might people be interested in hearing stories that include supernatural beings or supernatural events?

- Explore your feelings about trust. Have you ever trusted someone who eventually turned on you? Have you ever not trusted someone and later learned that you should have? Why is trust important in a relationship? There is a saying that it takes years to build up trust, and only seconds to destroy it. Do you agree? Why or why not?

- In most relationships, there is usually a dominant person. Think about your own relationships, either romantic or friendships. Who is the dominant person in your relationships? Are you the dominant person in one type of relationship, but not in another? What personality characteristics does the dominant person have? Do you choose to be the dominant person, or does that role naturally fall into place? Explain.

*During/after reading **Act Five***:

- Discuss the idea of "Fair is foul and foul is fair." Describe a time when something turned out differently than you expected, or a person seemed to be someone they were not.

- Do you believe in the idea of "an eye for an eye?" In other words, do you believe that people should receive the same punishment they put others through? Why or why not?

- If you had knowledge of what your own future held, how would your actions be affected? Do you think it is wise to know the future? Do you think it would change the person you are or how you live your life? What kinds of things would be different for you?

Macbeth

Glossary of Terms from Macbeth

The following is a comprehensive list of words and phrases found in Shakespeare's *Macbeth*. These are terms and expressions that audiences in Shakespeare's time would have had no problem understanding, however today, many of these words are out of use. It is also important to remember that Shakespeare is also credited with creating over 2,000 words! Making things even more confusing is that Shakespeare left out letters, replacing them with an apostrophe, left out words, and even rearranged word order. However, if you need help understanding what a word means, this list is here to help.

'gins: begins
'scaped: escaped
'tis: it is
'twas: it was
'twere: it were
'twixt: between
abide: to live or stay within
accursed: doomed; cursed
adieu: expression meaning "good bye"
afeard: afraid
alas: an expression of pity
an: if
anon: at once; soon
aright: in the correct or proper way
aroint: begone; get away
art: are
attend: listen; pay attention
aught: anything
avaunt: be gone!; go away!
avouch: attest to; vouch for
aweary: weary, tired
ay: yes
beest: be
beguile: deceive; cheat
behold: look; see
beldams: old hags
benison: blessing
bestows: puts something somewhere
bestride: step or walk
bind: link together
blasted: ruined; destroyed
borne: brought forth
bruited: spread rumors

cam'st: came
chid: chided; reprimanded; scolded
coign: a corner of a wall
couldst: could
crave: desire; wish for
deign: to accept; give in
didst: did
dispatch: to send away or to kill
doff: take off; remove
dost: do
doth: does
durst: past tense of *dare*
enkindle: arouse; excite
enow: enough
ere: before
fare thee well: Take care!
fee-grief: grief felt by only a few people
firstlings: first of its kind
folly: foolishness
gall: bitterness; resentment
get: give birth to
goodly: a substantial amount
hadst: had
hast: have or had
hath: have
heavy: sad
hellkite: fiendishly cruel person
hence: away from here; later
hereafter: after the present time
herein: in this document; in this case
hermits: those who pray for others
hie: go
hiss: mock; dismiss

hither: here
ho: an expression similar to "hey"
holp: past tense of help
hoodwink: trick or deceive
hurly-burly: confusion or commotion
kinsmen: family members; relatives
knell: slow bell ring
lave: wash; clean
lest: unless
liege: a feudal lord
limbeck: a substance that cleans or purifies
lo: look!
mark: listen; pay attention to
martlet: a small bird
mayst: may
measure: an amount
methinks: I think
mightst: might
mirth: laughter
missives: written orders
morrow: tomorrow
naught: nothing
nay: no
ne'er: never
niggard of your speech: stingy with your words—give details
nigh: near
nonpareil: something that is unparalleled
O: oh
o'erleap: overleap
oft'ner: more often
on't: on it
ope: open
perfect'st: most perfect
prate: silly chatter
prithee: request; ask
quit: get out of; go away
quoth: said
rapt: completely engrossed
retire: go to bed

seemeth: seems
shalt: shall; will
sirrah: fellow; young man
sooth: truth
th': the
thane: a baron in Scotland
thee: you
thence: away from there
therein: in that respect
therewithal: in addition to
thine: mine
thither: there
thou: you (informal)
thou'dst: you would
thou'rt: you are
thrice: three times
thy: your or my
thyself: yourself
tidings: news
till: until
tooth: subject of interest
twain: two
wail: mournful cry
wanton: growing quickly
weird: supernatural; not of the earth
whence: from what place?
wherefore: why
wherein: when; during which time
wherewith: with which
whiles: while
wilt: will
wit: desire
withal: with
wither: where
woe: grief
woeful: full of sadness
wooingly: favorably
would: wish
wouldst: would
wrought: full of
ye: plural form of you

Macbeth
List of Allusions

Act One

"cat i' th' adage": Lady Macbeth is referring to an old adage in which a cat wants to eat fish, but doesn't want to get her hands wet in the process. She is saying that Macbeth is being a coward by wanting to murder Duncan, but doesn't want to really be involved in the doing.

"I have begun to plant thee": biblical reference to Psalms 92: 12, 13, "The righteous shall flourish like the palm tree..." or Jeremiah 12:2, "You have planted them, and they will grow and bear fruit..."

"If it were done when 'tis done, then 'twere well / It were done quickly": refers to John 13: 27, Jesus told Judas, "What you are about to do, do quickly," sensing Judas's betrayal.

"insane root": possibly refers to hemlock, which, when eaten, causes madness

Aleppo: a city in Syria

Bellona's bridegroom: Bellona was the goddess of war

Golgotha: the biblical name for the place where Jesus was crucified

Graymalkin: a gray cat called upon in spell-making

kerns and galloglasses: Irish soldiers

limbeck: (also *alembeck*) a device used in the distillation of liquor; in this case, it is being used metaphorically, memory is being distilled—the guards will be so drunk, they will not be able to think straight

paddock: a toad used for spells

Saint Colme's Inch: an island near Edinburgh, Scotland

Tiger: the name of the husband's ship

Western Isles: Ireland

Act Two

"The Lord's anointed temple...stole thence the life o' th' building": reference to 1 Corinthians 3:17 "If any man defile the temple of God, him shall God destroy; for the temple of God is holy, which temple ye are."

"the primrose way to the everlasting bonfire": to be led down the "primrose way" is to be led astray or to be deceived by someone who is a hypocrite; the "everlasting bonfire" is a reference to hell.

Beelzebub: commonly translated as "the lord of the flies," the Philistine god Beelzebub is known as the prince of demons

equivocator: reference to Jesuit Henry Garnet, who was executed for his role in the Gunpowder Plot of 1605; wrote the "Treatise on Equivocation," which encouraged Catholics to speak ambiguously or, "equivocate" when they were being questioned by Protestant inquisitors so they wouldn't be persecuted for their religious beliefs.

farmer: well-known alias for Father Garnet of the Gunpowder Plot

Gorgon: a female supernatural creature, usually referring to any of three sisters who had hair made of venomous snakes

Hecate: the goddess of witchcraft

Neptune: the god of water and the sea in Roman mythology

Tarquin: the Roman Emperor Lucius Tarquinius Superbus was known for his tyranny over his empire, but was later successfully overthrown.

Act Three
"blood will have blood": a reference to Genesis 9:6, the story of Cain and Abel "Who so sheadeth man's blood, by man shall his blood be shed: for in the image of God hath he made man."

Caesar: Gaius Julius Caesar (July 13, 100 BC – March 15, 44 BC), Dictator of the Roman Republic, assassinated by his own senators

Mark Antony: a Roman philosopher and general; huge supporter and faithful friend of Julius Caesar

Act Four
"To offer up a weak, poor, innocent lamb, T' appease an angry god": the practice of sacrifice of an animal has been in existence for thousands of years, often in an attempt to please one of the gods of mythology

adder's fork: the forked tongue of a poisonous snake

blindworm: a legless lizard, with the body of a snake

eye of newt: the eye of a type of salamander

fillet of fenny: a slice of a type of swamp snake

gall of goat: the gallbladder of a goat

maw and gulf of ravined salt-sea shark: the jaw and stomach of a hungry saltwater shark

owlet's wing: the wing of a baby owl

tiger's chaudron: a tiger's intestines

Act Five
"Seyton! –I am sick at heart, / When I behold—Seyton, I say!": commonly believed to be a reference to Satan, as Macbeth has completely invoked the power of the devil to his purpose.

"Why should I play the Roman fool, and die / On mine own sword?": reference to the idea of Roman soldiers killing themselves with their own swords rather than facing defeat.

Macbeth
Vocabulary List

Act One
1. chalice
2. chastise
3. compunctious
4. dwindle
5. harbinger
6. implored
7. ingratitude
8. interim
9. mettle
10. minion
11. plight
12. prophetic
13. surmise
14. trifles
15. withered

Act Two
1. allegiance
2. augment
3. carousing
4. clamored
5. dire
6. gild
7. lamenting(s)
8. malice
9. palpable
10. parley
11. predominance
12. provoke
13. quenched
14. scruples
15. summons

Act Three
1. affliction
2. chide
3. cloistered
4. dauntless
5. fruitless
6. grapple
7. incensed
8. jovial
9. malevolence
10. pious
11. purged
12. scepter
13. sundry
14. tyrant
15. vile

Act Four
1. antic
2. avaricious
3. bodements
4. cistern
5. desolate
6. dolor
7. entrails
8. laudable
9. malady
10. pernicious
11. quarry
12. relish
13. resolute
14. sovereignty
15. teems

Act Five
1. agitation
2. arbitrate
3. condemn
4. divine
5. fortifies
6. fury
7. gentry
8. mar
9. murky
10. perturbation
11. pestered
12. pristine
13. recoil
14. revolts
15. upbraid

Name _____ Period _____

Macbeth
Act One
Scene Guide

For each act, you will be completing a Scene Guide to help you understand and follow the important elements of your reading. For each scene, complete each section fully, however, use short phrases or words to keep your note-taking short and succinct. The chart below will assist you in completing the activity. Act One, Scenes 1 and 2 have been completed for you as an example.

Example	
Characters	In this section, list the major characters who are a part of the action. It is not necessary to list minor characters who are not directly involved in the plot.
Action	In this section, list the important action that takes place in the scene.
Staging	What sets, furniture, or important props should be used in this scene to help establish the setting and/or action? Explain your choices.
Problem or Solution? How or Why?	Ask yourself whether this scene raises a problem or provides a solution to a previous problem. Almost all scenes will work in this way, either bringing up a problem or proposing a solution to some earlier problem. Sometimes, problem after problem is presented without a solution until the very end. Once you have decided, explain how or why you answered *problem* or *solution*. What issues are raised? Are some problems solved, and others still an issue? Explain your choice(s) here.

Scene One: An Open Field	
Characters	Three witches
Action	Three witches meet in an open field, speaking about a war that is almost over. They agree to meet again, upon the heath, with Macbeth present.
Staging	The "heath"; thunder, lightning—witches may be flying above a cauldron
Problem or Solution? How or Why?	We are not sure whether it is a problem yet, but they want to meet with Macbeth for some reason. Since this very short scene is the opening of the play, we are not sure what is to come. It begins the play with a dark sense of the unknown.

Scene Two: King Duncan's Camp at Forres	
Characters	King Duncan, Malcolm, the Captain, Lennox, Ross
Action	The Captain meets King Duncan and tells about Macbeth and the way he valiantly fought Macdonwald. He says it was a good fight. Macbeth slit Macdonwald down the middle, then cut off his head and stuck it on top of his sword. Ross announces they have won the battle. The King sends Ross to crown Macbeth the Thane of Cawdor.

| Staging | King's throne, good furniture, flags of Scotland; bloody Captain |
| Problem or Solution? How or Why? | Solution; Macbeth has helped Duncan and Scotland win the war against Norway, now Macbeth is being honored by Duncan by being promoted to the title of Thane of Cawdor. |

Scene Three: Upon the Heath

Characters	
Action	
Staging	
Problem or Solution? How or Why?	

Scene Four: Duncan's Camp at Forres

Characters	
Action	
Staging	
Problem or Solution? How or Why?	

Scene Five: Macbeth's Castle at Inverness

Characters	
Action	
Staging	

Problem or Solution? How or Why?	
Scene Six: Macbeth's Castle at Inverness	
Characters	
Action	
Staging	
Problem or Solution? How or Why?	
Scene Seven: Macbeth's Castle at Inverness	
Characters	
Action	
Staging	
Problem or Solution? How or Why?	

Now that you have read and taken notes on Act One, make a prediction about what you believe will happen next in the play.

My prediction: _____

_____

_____

Macbeth
Act One
Comprehension Check

Directions*: To give you a comprehensive understanding of all aspects of the play, answer the following questions using complete sentences on a separate sheet of paper. Be sure to use your Scene Guide to help you if you need it.*

Scene 1

1. When, where, and with whom do the witches plan to meet next?

Scene 2

1. Who does the Captain say is "brave"? What did this brave man do to deserve the title?

2. Who was he fighting against?

3. From where has Ross come? What news does he bring?

4. What did Ross say Scotland demanded from the King of Norway? What did they promise in return?

5. Who gains the title of Thane of Cawdor?

Scene 3

1. Summarize the story the first witch tells. What do the witches plan in revenge?

2. Why is Banquo confused by the witches when he first sees them?

3. When the witches first speak to Macbeth and Banquo, what do they say?

4. What do they prophesy for Banquo?

5. Why is Macbeth confused by the witches' prophecies?

6. Why have Ross and Angus come?

7. What does Macbeth mean when he says "Why do you address me in borrowed robes"? What does Angus tell Macbeth is the reason?

8. What does Macbeth mean by "the greatest is behind"?

9. In lines 127-129, Macbeth says "Two truths are told / as happy prologues to the swelling Act / Of the imperial theme." What "imperial theme" is he talking about? What are the "happy prologues"?

10. In his asides, (lines 130-142), what problems does Macbeth mention? What does he decide to do about his issue (lines 143-144)?

Scene 4

1. What do we learn at the beginning of this scene?

2. What does the King say about Cawdor?

3. Who gains the estate?

4. What is Macbeth's immediate reaction? What does Macbeth now feel he has to do?

5. What does Macbeth mean by "stars, hide your fires, / Let not light see my black and deep desires"? (lines 50-51)

Scene 5

1. Summarize what Macbeth tells his wife in his letter to her.

2. What is Lady Macbeth's reaction to this news?

3. What does Lady Macbeth say about her husband? Why is her description surprising, considering the description of Macbeth in Scene 2?

4. After she hears that Macbeth is on his way home and that the King is coming over (lines 33-53), what does Lady Macbeth want? What does she have planned?

5. What does she want Macbeth to do?

Scene 6

1. How does Duncan feel at the Macbeth estate? Why is this ironic?

Scene 7

1. In his soliloquy, Macbeth says "If it were done when 'tis done, then 'twere well if it were done quickly." What is "it"?

2. Why does Macbeth say Duncan is "here in double trust"? Why does this bother Macbeth?

3. Why does Macbeth second-guess the "deed"?

4. When Macbeth tries to call off the murder, what is Lady Macbeth's reaction?

5. When trying to convince Macbeth, Lady Macbeth says "I have given suck and know / How tender 'tis to love the babe that milks me; / I would while it was smiling in my face / Have plucked my nipple from his boneless gums / And dashed the brains out, had I so sworn as you / Have done to this." (lines 54-59) What is she saying? Why do you think she is being so dramatic?

6. What is Lady Macbeth's answer when Macbeth asks "if they fail"? (line 60)

7. What is the plan?

8. What is your impression of the relationship between Macbeth and Lady Macbeth? Why do you think Lady Macbeth has so much control over Macbeth?

9. Were Lady Macbeth's fears about Macbeth legitimate? Why or why not?

Name _____ Period _____

Macbeth
Act One
Standards Focus: Dialogue, Monologue, and More

By now, you should have read all or at least a good portion of Act One of *Macbeth*. Chances are, you may be finding the way Shakespeare wrote a bit confusing or even overwhelming. This exercise will take you through some of the unique aspects of dramatic literature: dialogue, soliloquies, monologues, asides, and stage directions. This will help you understand more about how dramatic literature is constructed, making it easier for you to understand the action of the play.

To review:
- **aside**: a "whispered" comment spoken directly to the audience—unheard by other characters
- **dialogue**: conversation between two or more characters
- **monologue**: a long speech spoken by a character to himself, another character, or to the audience
- **soliloquy**: thoughts spoken aloud by a character when he/she is alone, or thinks he/she is alone—talking to himself or herself
- **stage directions**: italicized comments that identify parts of the setting or the use of props or costumes, which give further information about a character or provide background information

Part A
Directions: *For each of the following quotes from Act One, a) identify the type of quote (aside, dialogue, monologue, soliloquy, or stage directions); b) describe the function and importance of this particular quote in the context of the play. Scene and line numbers have been given so that you can use your text for help. Two examples have been done for you.*

Ex 1. (Scene 2)
Alarum within. Enter King (Duncan), Malcolm, Donalbain, Lennox, with Attendants, meeting a bleeding Captain.
   a. stage directions
   b. These stage directions give the actors and director directions about who should enter, possibly in which order, and whether they should have props. In this case, the stage director/stage hands know that they need to sound the alarm announcing the King's arrival, and that they are meeting with a bloodied soldier.

Ex 2. (Scene 3, Lines 116-120)
Macbeth:
   [Aside] Glamis, and Thane of Cawdor – The greatest is behind.
   [To Ross and Angus] Thanks for your pains.
   [Aside to Banquo] Do you not hope your children shall be kings,
   When those that gave the Thane of Cawdor to me
   Promised no less to them?
   a. asides
   b. In this excerpt, there are a lot of specific directions given to Macbeth. First, he speaks an aside that only the audience can hear. He then thanks Ross and Angus

directly, and then speaks closely in an aside that only Banquo (and the audience) can hear.

1. (Scene 3, Lines 52-61)
    Banquo:
    [To the witches] I' th' name of truth
    Are ye fantastical, or that indeed
    Which outwardly ye show? My noble partner
    You greet with present grace and great prediction
    Of noble having and of royal hope,
    That he seems rapt withal. To me you speak not.
    If you can look into the seeds of time
    And say which grain will grow and which will not,
    Speak then to me, who neither beg nor fear
    Your favors nor your hate.

    a. _____

    b. _____
    _____
    _____
    _____

2. (Scene 3, Lines 127-137)
    Macbeth:
    [Aside] Two truths are told,
    As happy prologues to the swelling act
    Of the imperial theme. –I thank you, gentlemen.—
    [Aside] This supernatural soliciting
    Cannot be ill, cannot be good. If ill,
    Why hath it given me earnest of success
    Commencing in a truth? I am Thane of Cawdor.
    If good, why do I yield to that suggestion
    Whose horrid image doth unfix my hair
    And make my seated heart knock at my ribs
    Against the use of nature?

    a. _____

    b. _____
    _____
    _____

3. (Scene 5)
    Enter Macbeth's Wife, alone, with a letter.

    a. _____

    b. _____
    _____
    _____

4. (Scene 5, Lines 37-42)
   Lady Macbeth:
       The raven himself is hoarse
       That croaks the fatal entrance of Duncan
       Under my battlements. Come, you spirits
       That tend on mortal thoughts, unsex me here,
       And fill me from the crown to the topful
       Of direst cruelty

   a. _____

   b. _____

   _____

   _____

5. (Scene 5, Lines 58-60)
   Macbeth: My dearest love,
       Duncan comes here tonight.
   Lady Macbeth: And when goes hence?
   Macbeth: Tomorrow, as he purposes.
   Lady Macbeth: O, never
       Shall sun that morrow see.

   a. _____

   b. _____

   _____

   _____

Part B
Directions*: Using the text of Act One, find, identify, and explain one example of each of the following: aside, dialogue, monologue, soliloquy, and stage directions. Write your answers on a separate page and attach it to this worksheet. Be sure to include the excerpt from the play, the type of example, and an explanation of what is happening in the excerpt, similar to the work you did in Part A.*

Part C
Directions*: Answer the following questions using complete sentences on your separate piece of paper.*

1. Why do you think Shakespeare has written in so many asides in this act? What effect do you think the asides might have on the audience?

2. In your own words, explain the difference between monologues and soliloquies.

3. Why do you think Shakespeare did not include more details in the stage directions, i.e. why didn't he include when a character walks across the stage or sits down, etc.?

4. How can you tell the difference between an aside and a soliloquy?

Name _____ Period _____

Macbeth
Act One
Standards Focus: Mood

Mood is the atmosphere or emotional state created by a piece of literature. The words and sentence structure that a writer uses can contribute to the mood of a piece of work. Shakespeare immediately creates a mood of mystery and fear from the very first moment the witches appear on stage in Act One.

Mood is *usually* described in expressions of feeling and emotions, such as *fear, anger, hatred, unease, loneliness, confusion* or *jealousy*, to name a few. It is the feeling a reader gets from reading the text. To help identify the mood, ask yourself, "How does Shakespeare want me to **feel** after reading this (line, passage, scene, etc.)?

*First, list 10 different **moods** (do not use the ones that have already been mentioned) in the space below. Challenge yourself to avoid "happy" and "sad" and to find better adjectives such as "ecstatic" or "gloomy."*

_____   _____

_____   _____

_____   _____

_____   _____

_____   _____

Part A
Directions: *For the following excerpts from Act One, use your list to help you identify the mood that Shakespeare is attempting to create. Also, underline the words (context clues) from the quote that contribute to the mood. An example has been done for you.*

Ex. "Fair is <u>foul</u> and <u>foul</u> is fair. / Hover through the <u>fog</u> and <u>filthy air</u>." (Sc. 1; 12-13)
Mood(s) created: <u>dark, mysterious, ominous, depressing</u>

1. "For brave Macbeth (well he deserves that name), / Disdaining Fortune, with his brandished steel, / Which smoked with bloody executions / Like valor's minion, carved out his passage / Till he faced the slave" (Sc. 2; 18-22)

   Mood(s) created: _____

2. "I am Thane of Cawdor: / If good, why do I yield to that suggestion / Whose horrid image doth unfix my hair, / And make my seated heart knock at my ribs, / Against the use of nature?" (Sc. 3; 133-137)

   Mood(s) created: _____

3. "Oh worthiest cousin, / The sin of my ingratitude even now / Was heavy on me! Thou art so far before / That swiftest wing of recompense is slow / To overtake thee." (Sc. 4; 17-21)

   Mood(s) created: _____

4. "Stars hide your fires! / Let not light see my black and deep desires. / The eye wink at the hand; yet let that be, / Which the eye fears, when it is done, to see." (Sc. 4; 58-61)

   Mood(s) created: _____

5. "Come, you spirits / That tend on mortal thoughts, unsex me here, / And fill me from the crown to the toe top-full / Of direst cruelty!" (Sc. 5; 38-41)

   Mood(s) created: _____

6. "This castle hath a pleasant seat. The air / Nimbly and sweetly recommends itself / Unto our gentle senses." (Sc. 6; 1-3)

   Mood(s) created: _____

Part B

1. What mood(s) seem to permeate the majority of Act One? _____

   _____

   _____

2. What happens in this act that makes these moods appropriate? _____

   _____

   _____

   _____

   _____

3. What scene(s) or parts of scenes change the mood of the play so far? How does Shakespeare accomplish these changes in mood? In your opinion, how do these changes in mood contribute to the story so far? _____

   _____

   _____

   _____

   _____

   _____

   _____

   _____

   _____

   _____

Macbeth
Act One
Assessment Preparation: Context Clues

In most assessments, you must infer (make an educated guess) the meanings of words by looking at context clues, or clues within an entire line, sentence, or paragraph. You must look at how the word is used in order to make an inference.

Part A
Directions: *For each of the following vocabulary words from Act One, first indicate the part of speech in which the vocabulary word in **bold** appears (noun, verb, etc.) in the lines from the text. Then provide a synonym for the vocabulary word based upon the clues. (If you need further clarification, read a few lines before and after the vocabulary word). For c., look up the word and write down the dictionary definition. How accurate is your inference? For d., now that you know the correct definition, explain how the context clues aid (or don't aid) you in understanding the meaning of the sentence.*

Ex. King Duncan: *What bloody man is that? He can report, / As seemeth by his **plight**, of the revolt/ The newest state.* (Sc. 1)

  a. Part of Speech: ___noun_____

  b. Synonym based on Inference: __appearance_

  c. Definition: n. a difficult or dangerous situation or predicament

  d. Explanation: I can see that I was just assuming that because he was bloody, Duncan was referring to the blood on him. Since plight refers to the situation he has been in, I can see that Duncan is referring to everything the man has been through (i.e. the battle).

1. Captain: *For brave Macbeth – well he deserves that name – / Disdaining Fortune, with his brandished steel, / Which smoked with bloody execution, / Like valor's **minion** carved out his passage / Till he faced the slave* (Sc. 2)

  a. Part of Speech: _____

  b. Synonym based on Inference: _____

  c. Definition: _____

    _____

  d. Explanation: _____

    _____

2. First Witch: *Weary sev'nights, nine times nine, / Shall he **dwindle**, peak, and pine.* (Sc. 3)

  a. Part of Speech: _____

  b. Synonym based on Inference: _____

  c. Definition: _____

Name _____ Period _____

   d. Explanation: _____

      _____

      _____

3. Banquo: *What are these, / So **withered** and so wild in their attire / That look not like the' inhabitants o' th' earth / And yet are on 't?* (Sc. 3)

   a. Part of Speech: _____

   b. Synonym based on Inference: _____

   c. Definition: _____

      _____

   d. Explanation: _____

      _____

4. Macbeth: *Say from whence / You owe this strange intelligence, or why / Upon this blasted heath you stop our way / With such **prophetic** greeting.* (Sc. 3)

   a. Part of Speech: _____

   b. Synonym based on Inference: _____

   c. Definition: _____

      _____

   d. Explanation: _____

      _____

5. Banquo: *But 'tis strange; /And oftentimes, to win us to our harm, / The instruments of darkness tell us truths, / Win us with honest **trifles**, to betray 's / In deepest consequence.* (Sc. 3)

   a. Part of Speech: _____

   b. Synonym based on Inference: _____

   c. Definition: _____

      _____

   d. Explanation: _____

      _____

      _____

6. Macbeth: *My thought, whose murder is but fantastical, / Shakes so my single state of man that function / Is smothered in **surmise** and nothing is but what is not.* (Sc. 3)

   a. Part of Speech: _____

   b. Synonym based on Inference: _____

   c. Definition: _____

      _____

    d. Explanation: _____

_____

_____

Part B

Directions: *For each of the following vocabulary words from Act One, look up the word in bold and write down the dictionary definition. For b., now that you know the correct definition, explain how the context clues aid (or don't aid) you in understanding the meaning of the sentence.*

1. Macbeth: *Think upon what hath chanced, and at more time, / The* **interim** *having weighed it, let us speak / Our free hearts each to other.* (Sc. 4)

    a. Definition: _____

    _____

    b. Explanation: _____

    _____

    _____

2. Malcolm: *But I have spoke / With one that saw him die, who did report / That very frankly he confessed his treasons,* **implored** *your highness' pardon, and set forth / A deep repentance.* (Sc. 4)

    a. Definition: _____

    _____

    b. Explanation: _____

    _____

    _____

3. Duncan: *O worthiest cousin / The sin of my* **ingratitude** *even now / Was heavy on me.* (Sc. 4)

    a. Definition: _____

    _____

    b. Explanation: _____

    _____

    _____

4. Macbeth: *I'll be myself the* **harbinger**, *and make joyful / The hearing of my wife with your approach; / So, humbly take my leave.* (Sc. 4)

    a. Definition: _____

    _____

b. Explanation: _____
   _____
   _____

5. Lady Macbeth: *Hie thee hither, / That I may pour my spirits in thine ear / And* **chastise** *with the valor of my tongue / All that impedes thee from the golden round / Which fate and metaphysical aid doth seem / To have thee crowned withal.* (Sc. 5)

   a. Definition: _____
      _____

   b. Explanation: _____
      _____
      _____

6. Lady Macbeth: *Make thick my blood; / Stop up th' access and passage to remorse, / That no* **compunctious** *visitings of nature / Shake my fell purpose nor keep peace between / Th' effect and it.* (Sc. 5)

   a. Definition: _____
      _____

   b. Explanation: _____
      _____
      _____

7. Macbeth: *This evenhanded justice / Commends th' ingredients of our poisoned* **chalice** */ To our own lips.* (Sc. 7)

   a. Definition: _____
      _____

   b. Explanation: _____
      _____
      _____

8. Macbeth: *Bring forth men-children only; / For thy undaunted* **mettle** *should compose / Nothing but males.* (Sc. 7)

   a. Definition: _____
      _____

   b. Explanation: _____
      _____
      _____

Macbeth
Act Two
Scene Guide

Scene One: Macbeth's Castle at Inverness	
Characters	
Action	
Staging	
Problem or Solution? How or Why?	
Scene Two: Macbeth's Castle	
Characters	
Action	
Staging	
Problem or Solution? How or Why?	
Scene Three: Macbeth's Castle	
Characters	
Action	

Staging	
Problem or Solution? How or Why?	

Scene Four: Outside Macbeth's Castle	
Characters	
Action	
Staging	
Problem or Solution? How or Why?	

Now that you have read and taken notes on Act Two, make a prediction about what you believe will happen next in the play.

My prediction: _____

_____

_____

Macbeth
Act Two
Comprehension Check

Directions: *To give you a comprehensive understanding of all aspects of the play, answer the following questions using complete sentences on a separate sheet of paper. Be sure to use your Scene Guide to help you.*

Scene One

1. About what time is it at the beginning of this Act?

2. Why can't Banquo sleep?

3. What did the King give Lady Macbeth? What kind of mood was the King in before he went to bed?

4. What lie does Macbeth tell Banquo?

5. What does Macbeth "see"?

6. In his soliloquy, what lines indicate that Macbeth has been having nightmares?

7. What does the bell indicate?

Scene Two

1. What does Lady Macbeth mean by "That which hath made them drunk hath made me bold" (line 1)

2. Why does Lady say she couldn't murder Duncan herself?

3. What happened to spook Macbeth while he waited to kill Duncan?

4. What does Macbeth then think he hears? Why do you think he "hears" this?

5. What mistake does Macbeth make?

6. How does Lady fix his mistake?

7. What evidence from the murder upsets Macbeth the most?

8. Lady Macbeth says "A little water clears us of this deed, how easy is it then!" (lines 70-71) Is this true? How does this seem like an understatement?

9. What line reveals that Macbeth is now regretting what they have done?

Scene Three

1. This scene with the Porter provides some comic relief. Why is this scene important to the audience at this time?

2. What is ironic about his statement "but this place is too cold for hell"?

3. According to the Porter, how is drink an "equivocator of lechery"?

Name _____ Period _____

4. Why is Macduff up so early?

5. Explain why Lennox said the night was "unruly." (line 53)

6. Who found Duncan's body?

7. What does Macbeth confess to Macduff? What does he give as the reason he did it?

8. What is Lady Macbeth's reaction to hearing this? Do you think her reaction is sincere?

9. What do Malcolm and Donalbain decide to do? Why?

Scene Four

1. What strange events have been happening?

2. Who have become suspects in Duncan's murder? Why?

Name _____ Period _____

Macbeth
Act Two
Standards Focus: Figurative Language

One of the most captivating aspects of *Macbeth* is Shakespeare's use of the literary device called **figurative language**—words that are used to convey images beyond their literal sense. There are several types of figurative language, also called **figures of speech**:

- **metaphor** — a comparison made between two unlike objects
- **simile** – a comparison between two unlike objects using the words "like" or "as"
- **personification** – giving human qualities or characteristics to non-human objects
- **hyperbole** – truth exaggerated for humor or emphasis

Directions*: Read each excerpt from Acts One and Two. For Part A, decide what type of figure of speech has been underlined. Then, for Part b, "Analysis," identify the comparison being made, the object being personified, or the effect of the exaggeration. The numbers in parentheses represent the act and scene in which the quote appears. An example has been done for you.*

Ex. If I say sooth, I must report they were / <u>As cannons overcharged with double cracks</u> (1.2)

    a. Figure of Speech: <u>simile</u>

    b. Analysis: <u>the soldiers were on a rampage, ready to fight their way through anything and everything to win the battle</u>

1. If you can look into the <u>seeds of time / And say which grain will grow and which will not,</u> Speak then to me (1.3)

    a. Figure of Speech: _____

    b. Analysis: _____

    _____

2. If chance will have me king, why, <u>chance may crown me</u> / Without my stir. (1.3)

    a. Figure of Speech: _____

    b. Analysis: _____

    _____

3. Come what come may, / <u>Time and the hour runs through the roughest day.</u> (1. 3)

    a. Figure of Speech: _____

    b. Analysis: _____

    _____

4. <u>More is thy due than more than all can pay.</u> (1. 4)

    a. Figure of Speech: _____

    b. Analysis: _____

    _____

5. That my (A) <u>keen knife see not the wound it makes</u>, / Nor (B) <u>heaven peep through</u> the (C) <u>blanket of the dark</u>, To cry, 'Hold, hold!' (1. 5)

    (A) a. Figure of Speech: _____

        b. Analysis: _____

        _____

    (B) a. Figure of Speech: _____

        b. Analysis: _____

        _____

    (C) a. Figure of Speech: _____

        b. Analysis: _____

        _____

6. I have no <u>spur to prick the sides of my intent, which o'erleaps itself and falls on th' other</u>– (1.7)

    a. Figure of Speech: _____

    b. Analysis: _____

    _____

7. A heavy summons lies <u>like lead upon me</u>, / And yet I would not sleep. (2.1)

    a. Figure of Speech: _____

    b. Analysis: _____

    _____

8. Methought I heard a voice cry "Sleep no more! / <u>Macbeth does murder sleep</u>" (2.2)

    a. Figure of Speech: _____

    b. Analysis: _____

    _____

9. <u>Will all great Neptune's ocean wash this blood /Clean from my hand? No, this my hand will rather / The multitudinous seas incarnadine, / Making the green one red</u>. (2. 2)

    a. Figure of Speech: _____

    b. Analysis: _____

    _____

10. Most sacrilegious <u>murder hath broke ope / The Lord's anointed temple and stole thence / The life o' th' building!</u> (2.3)

    a. Figure of Speech: _____

    b. Analysis: _____

    _____

Name _____ Period _____

Macbeth
Act Two
Standards Focus: Plot and Conflict

Plot is the related series of events that make up a story. In other words, plot is the action that occurs as the story progresses. There are several parts of a plot:

- **exposition** - the beginning of the story that gives background information on characters and previous action
- **rising action** - the beginning of the action that will lead to a high point (climax) in the story
- **climax** - the turning point of the story; the part of the story in which the protagonist reaches an emotional high point or a peak in power
- **falling action** - the action that occurs after the climax
- **resolution** (also **dénouement** [**day – new – mawh**]) - the ending of the story; or when all loose ends are tied up and problems are (generally) solved

Part A
Directions: By Act Two, the exposition and rising action of the play have been presented, leading to the climax of the play, which begins to develop late in Act Two. Below are important events of Acts One—Two of Macbeth. Arrange the events in chronological order (the order in which they occurred) on the lines below the plot events. HINT: USE A PENCIL IN CASE YOU MAKE A MISTAKE AND NEED TO FIX SOMETHING! The first event has been done for you.

Duncan's sons flee, and are blamed for the king's murder.
King Duncan announces that Macbeth will be the new Thane of Cawdor.
Lady Macbeth drugs Duncan's servants.
Lady Macbeth learns about the witches' prophecies.
Lady Macbeth takes the daggers to place them on the king's men and hide her husband's deed.
Macbeth is to be named the new King of Scotland.
Macbeth murders Duncan.
Macbeth sees the imaginary dagger leading him to kill the king.
Macbeth tells everyone that he killed the king's men for what they had done.
Macduff finds the murdered king.
~~The Captain tells King Duncan how bravely and nobly Macbeth fought Macdonwald.~~
The King announces Malcolm will become the King's successor.
The Witches tell Macbeth that he will become Thane of Cawdor and king.

Events in Chronological Order:

1. The Captain tells King Duncan how bravely and nobly Macbeth fought Macdonwald.

2. _____

3. _____

4. _____

5. _____

6. _____

7. _____

8. _____

9. _____

10. _____

11. _____

12. _____

13. _____

Part B

Within the plot, there is also **conflict**. Conflict is a struggle between opposing forces, and can be between a man and his conscience, man and another man (or woman), or man against nature, such as weather or the environment. If conflict is written well, it can create a feeling of suspense, tension, and intrigue.

There are several types of conflict:
1. **man versus man**—struggle between two or more characters
2. **man versus himself**—struggle between a character and his conscience, morals, or physical limitations
3. **man versus nature**—struggle between a character and a force of nature such as weather or the environment
4. **man versus society**—struggle between a character and the rules, beliefs, or pressures of a society or community
5. **man versus fate**—struggle between a character and the forces of the universe, such as God, destiny, or chance happenings

In addition, conflict can be divided into external or internal conflicts. **External conflicts** are man versus man, man versus nature, man versus society, and man versus fate. The **internal conflict** is man versus himself.

Directions: *For each of the following events from Acts One-Two, decide who or what is involved in the conflict, and which type of conflict is being represented, and whether it is internal or external conflict. Finally, explain how you feel this conflict will ultimately affect the events of the play. An example has been done for you.*

Ex. The King announces Malcolm will become the King's successor.
   a. Opposing forces: _Malcolm versus Macbeth_____
   b. Type of conflict: _man versus man_____

    c. Explanation: <u>It is at this point, when Duncan announces Malcolm as his successor,</u> <u>that Macbeth knows Malcolm must be "removed" from the equation so that Macbeth</u> <u>can be king.</u>

1. In Act One, Macbeth hears the witches' prophecies that he will be Thane of Cawdor and then king.

    a. Opposing forces: _____

    b. Type of conflict: _____

    c. Explanation: _____

    _____

    _____

2. In Act One, Lady Macbeth fears that Macbeth is too weak and ineffectual to go after what the witches have predicted.

    a. Opposing forces: _____

    b. Type of conflict: _____

    c. Explanation: _____

    _____

    _____

3. In Act One, Macbeth says that he has no reason, other than his own ambitions, to kill the king.

    a. Opposing forces: _____

    b. Type of conflict: _____

    c. Explanation: _____

    _____

    _____

4. At the end of Act One, Macbeth has doubts while Lady Macbeth calls him a coward, urging him to kill the king.

    a. Opposing forces: _____

    b. Type of conflict: _____

    c. Explanation: _____

    _____

    _____

5. After Macbeth murders Duncan in Act Two, he is so horrified at what he has done that he forgets to plant the daggers on the king's men.

    a. Opposing forces: _____

    b. Type of conflict: _____

    c. Explanation: _____

    _____

    _____

Macbeth
Act Two
Assessment Preparation: Word Usage

Directions: *Answer each of the following questions based on the vocabulary words from Act Two. The answer may be the vocabulary word itself, or it may be a short response based upon the use of the vocabulary word. An answer may be used more than once.*

allegiance	augment	carousing	clamored
dire	gild	lamenting	malice
palpable	parley	predominance	provoke
quenched	scruples	summons	

1. Which word concerns a deep loyalty towards someone or something? _____

2. How are *carousing* and *lamenting* opposites? _____
    _____

3. Which word belongs in this group? *conscience, principles, ethics,* _____

4. Which word is an antonym of diminish? _____

5. Which word could be used to describe what you feel when you are extremely thirsty and
    finally get to drink a glass of water? _____

6. Name two things that may be or appear *gilded*. _____
    _____

7. What things might *provoke* a dog to attack? _____
    _____

8. Which word might describe the feeling between sworn enemies? _____

9. Which is worse—a *dire* situation or a critical problem? Explain your answer. _____
    _____

10. Which of the following words would NOT be considered a synonym of the word
    palpable? tangible, immaterial, physical, blatant, overt, flagrant, doubtful, ethereal
    _____

11. If your mother asked you to *parley*, what would you be doing? _____
    _____

12. Which vocabulary word comes from the Latin root, *dominus*, meaning *master*?
    _____

13. Which word applies to each of the following: *a witch calling upon her spirits; a court
    document; a note calling you to the Principal's office?*_____

14. The teenagers _____ to catch a glimpse of, or get an autograph from,
    the pop star before his show.

Name _____ Period _____

Macbeth
Act Three
Scene Guide

Scene One: Castle at Forres	
Characters	
Action	
Staging	
Problem or Solution? How or Why?	
Scene Two: A Room in the Castle	
Characters	
Action	
Staging	
Problem or Solution? How or Why?	
Scene Three: Outside the Castle	
Characters	
Action	
Staging	
Problem or Solution? How or Why?	

Scene Four: The Great Hall of the Castle	
Characters	
Action	
Staging	
Problem or Solution? How or Why?	
Scene Five: The Forest	
Characters	
Action	
Staging	
Problem or Solution? How or Why?	
Scene Six: The Castle at Forres	
Characters	
Action	
Staging	
Problem or Solution? How or Why?	

Now that you have read and taken notes on Act Three, make a prediction about what you believe will happen next in the play.

My prediction: _____

_____

Macbeth
Act Three
Comprehension Check

Directions: *To give you a comprehensive understanding of all aspects of the play, answer the following questions using complete sentences on a separate sheet of paper. Be sure to use your Scene Guide to help you.*

Scene One

1. What suspicion about Macbeth does Banquo reveal in his soliloquy?

2. What is Banquo hoping for?

3. What does Macbeth say the "bloody cousins" (Malcolm and Donalbain) are up to?

4. For what reasons does Macbeth want Banquo murdered?

5. What reason does Macbeth give for not killing Banquo himself?

6. When does Macbeth want Banquo and Fleance killed?

7. How are Macbeth's fears justified in this scene?

Scene Two

1. What lines reveal how Lady Macbeth is feeling about being queen?

2. What is Lady Macbeth's problem with Macbeth?

3. What does Macbeth mean by "Be innocent of the knowledge, dearest chuck / Till thou applaud the deed"?

Scene Three

1. What does the second murderer mean when he says "We have lost / Best half of our affair"?

2. Some scholars believe that the third murderer might be Macbeth himself. Draw an argument as to whether Macbeth would participate in the murder or not. Give reasons for your position.

Scene Four

1. How does Macbeth react to the news that Fleance escaped?

2. Macbeth's sightings have gotten worse, as he insists he sees Banquo's ghost. How might this progression be a reflection of Macbeth's mental state?

3. What explanation does Lady Macbeth give for Macbeth's behavior?

4. How does Lady Macbeth try to calm Macbeth down?

5. What is your explanation for the appearance of Banquo's ghost at the table? Why do you think Macbeth is the only one who can see him?

6. Besides Banquo, who was conspicuously absent from the banquet?

7. Many scholars consider scene four to be the climax of the play. Find one or two lines from this scene that could be the indicator that the climax of the play has been reached, and explain your reason for this choice.

Scene Five

1. Scholars believe that scene five was not written by Shakespeare, but was added later. Why do you think this scene was added at this point? (Consider what has just happened in the play.)

2. Why is Hecate angry?

3. What does Hecate say will soon be coming?

4. What do you think Hecate means when she says "And you all know security / Is mortals' chiefest enemy"? Do you agree? Why or why not?

5. Some producers/directors often omit this scene from their productions. Do you think removing this scene would change the play? Why or why not?

Scene Six

1. What things does Lennox say have been "strangely borne"?

2. What have Malcolm and Macduff been up to?

Macbeth
Act Three
Standards Focus: Irony

Irony is an inconsistency between appearance and reality. There are several types of irony:

- **Verbal** irony is when a speaker or writer says one thing but actually means the opposite. For example, when your mom walks into your filthy bedroom and says, "I see you've cleaned your room!" Sarcasm, overstatement (also called hyperbole), and understatement, are all types of verbal irony.

- **Situational** irony is when the outcome of a situation is inconsistent with what we expect would logically or normally occur. An example of situational irony would be if a thief's house was broken into at the same time he was robbing someone's house.

- **Dramatic** irony is when the audience or the reader is aware of something that a character does not know. For example: When King Duncan visits Macbeth's castle, he comments on how welcoming the home is, and how comfortable he feels. We as the audience know that King Duncan should feel anything but comfortable, as he is about to be murdered. The use of dramatic irony helps increase the tension and excitement of the play, and draws the audience more deeply into the story.

*Directions: For the following excerpts from Acts One through Three, Shakespeare effectively uses **dramatic irony** to intrigue the reader and deepen the impact of the consequences the characters ultimately face. For each of the following examples of dramatic irony, explain what the audience knows that the characters do not.*

1. The Thane of Cawdor was just executed and the King feels foolish for having trusted him: "He was a gentleman on whom I built / An absolute trust." Later, Macbeth is named the new Thane of Cawdor.

   What the audience knows: _____

   _____

   _____

2. After the murder of Duncan, the porter of the castle wakes up and responds to the knocking at the door. He complains about the cold, saying that "this place is too cold for Hell."

   What the audience knows: _____

   _____

   _____

3. In his monologue in Act Three, Scene I, Macbeth says it was because of the weird sisters' predictions that he murdered Banquo.

   What the audience knows: _____

   _____

   _____

Name _____ Period _____

4. Lennox says, "It was for Malcolm and Donalbain / To kill their gracious father? Damned fact! / How it did grieve Macbeth!"

   What the audience knows: _____

   _____

   _____

5. Macbeth is the only character to see Banquo's ghost. He is stricken with fear and collapses.

   What the audience knows: _____

   _____

   _____

6. In Act Three, Lady Macbeth complains that she is not feeling very comfortable in her new role as Queen. "Naught's had, all's spent, / Where our desire is got without content. / 'Tis safer to be that which we destroy / Than by destruction dwell in doubtful joy."

   What the audience knows: _____

   _____

   _____

7. At the beginning of Act Three, Macbeth asks Banquo whether he is going for a ride in the afternoon, and whether Fleance will be joining him.

   What the audience knows: _____

   _____

   _____

8. At the banquet in Act Three, Macbeth proclaims "I drink to th' general joy o' th' whole table, / And to our dear friend Banquo, whom we miss. / Would he were here!"

   What the audience knows: _____

   _____

   _____

9. Why do you think authors like Shakespeare employ the use of irony in their work? How does the use of irony contribute to the enjoyment of the text? _____

   _____

   _____

   _____

   _____

   _____

Name _____ Period _____

Macbeth
Act Three
Standards Focus: Characterization

Characterization is the technique by which authors develop characters. **Direct characterization** is when the author or narrator directly tells the reader what the character is like. For example, "Jennifer is a good student." The author wants us to know this detail about Jennifer, and does not give us the chance to take a guess about this aspect of her personality.

In drama, since the action of the play is written in dialogue form, there is little direct characterization. If the author wants you to know something concrete through direct characterization, it may appear in the stage directions. However, for the most part, anything you need to know about a character in a play is spoken by either the character himself or by other characters, which leads us to the concept of *indirect characterization*.

Indirect characterization is when the author gives information about a character and allows the reader to draw his or her own conclusions about that character. Two of the ways we can learn about a character through indirect characterization are:

- *Through the character's own thoughts, feelings and actions*— the reader witnesses what the character does or says, and learns something about the character from these thoughts, feelings, or actions. For example, "On her way to class after lunch, Susan saw some trash on the ground that wasn't hers. She decided to pick it up anyway, and threw it in the trash can."

  The reader can make some assumptions about Susan from this excerpt: she cares about the environment, she takes pride in her school, she likes things neat and tidy, etc. All of these are appropriate assumptions based on Susan's *actions*.

- *Through interactions with other characters*— the reader witnesses the interactions between characters, including how other characters treat or react to another character, and what they say and do towards one another. For example:

  "Maggie said, 'Julie seems not to care about her school work anymore. It's as if she is distracted or concerned about something. What do you think?'
  'I don't know, but it is certainly unlike her to get bad grades,' Kamesha replied."

  The reader can make assumptions about Julie from this conversation between Maggie and Kamesha. The reader can conclude that Julie used to work hard and get good grades in school, that she may be distracted about something, and that she is not behaving like her usual self.

Part One: What Characters Say/Infer About Themselves

Directions: To help you learn more about the characters in Macbeth, *examine each of the following excerpts from Acts One-Three. For each excerpt, explain what we learn about the character and why this particular selection is important to the story so far. Act and scene numbers have been given to help with the context of the excerpt. An example has been done for you.*

Ex. Macbeth: *Is this a dagger I see before me, / The handle toward my hand? Come, let me clutch thee. / I have thee not, and yet I see thee still. / Art thou not, fatal vision, sensible /*

To feeling as to sight? Or art though but / A dagger of the mind, a false creation / Proceeding from the heat-oppressed brain? ... Mine eyes are made the fools o' th' other senses, / Or else worth all the rest. I see thee still, / And on thy blade and dudgeon gouts of blood, / which was not so before. There's no such thing. / It is the bloody business which informs thus to mine eyes. (Act II, Scene 1)

   a. What we learn about Macbeth: <u>Macbeth must murder Duncan, but is clearly starting to have second thoughts about it. He begins to lose his mind a bit as he envisions a bloody dagger leading him to kill Duncan.</u>

   b. Why it is important to the story so far: <u>This is the first time that we see how the idea of the murder is starting to affect Macbeth. At this point, he has a conscience, and knows that what he is doing is not right. He knows there are supernatural, or at least evil, influences involved.</u>

1. Duncan: *There's no art / To find the mind's construction in the face. / He was a gentleman on whom I built an absolute trust.* (Act I, Scene 4)

   a. What we learn about Duncan: _____

   _____

   b. Why it is important to the story so far: _____

   _____

   _____

2. Lady Macbeth: *Your hand, your tongue; look like the innocent flower, / But be the serpent under 't. He that's coming / Must be provided for; and you shall put / This night's great business into my dispatch, / Which shall to all our nights and days to come / Give solely sovereign sway and masterdom.* (Act I, Scene 5)

   a. What we learn about Lady Macbeth: _____

   _____

   b. Why it is important to the story so far: _____

   _____

   _____

3. Macbeth: *What hands are here? Ha! They pluck out mine eyes. / Will all great Neptune's ocean wash this blood / Clean from my hand? No, this my hand will rather / The multitudinous seas incarnadine, / Making the green one red.* (Act II, Scene 2)

   a. What we learn about Macbeth: _____

   _____

   b. Why it is important to the story so far: _____

   _____

   _____

4. Banquo: *If there come truth from them– / as upon thee, Macbeth, their speeches shine– / Why, by the verities on thee made good, / May they not be my oracles as well? / And set me up in hope?* (Act III, Scene 1)

    a. What we learn about Banquo: _____

    _____

    b. Why it is important to the story so far: _____

    _____

    _____

Part Two: What Characters Say/Infer About Other Characters

Directions: *For each excerpt, explain what we learn about the character(s) and why this particular selection is important to the story so far. Act and scene numbers have been given to help with the context of the excerpt.*

1. Captain: *For brave Macbeth (well he deserves that name), / Disdaining Fortune, with his brandished steel, / Which smoked with bloody executions / Like valor's minion, carved out his passage / Till he faced the slave* (Act I, Scene 2)

    a. What we learn about Macbeth: _____

    _____

    b. Why it is important to the story so far: _____

    _____

    _____

2. Banquo: *What are these, / So withered and so wild in their attire / That look not like th' inhabitants o' th' earth / And yet are on 't? ... You should be women, / And yet your beards forbid me to interpret / That you are so.* (Act I, Scene 3)

    a. What we learn about the witches: _____

    _____

    c. Why it is important to the story so far: _____

    _____

    _____

3. Lady Macbeth: *Glamis thou art, and Cawdor, and shalt be / What thou art promised. Yet I do fear thy nature. / It is too full o' th' milk of human kindness / To catch the nearest way. Thou wouldst be great, / Art not without ambition, but without the illness should attend it.* (Act I, Scene 5)

    a. What we learn about Macbeth: _____

    _____

    b. Why it is important to the story so far: _____

    _____

    _____

Name _____ Period _____

Macbeth
Act Three
Assessment Preparation: Vocabulary Builders

Directions: *Choose ONE of the following activities below to learn the vocabulary words from Act Three. The vocabulary words are listed below.*

affliction	grapple	purged
chide	incensed	scepter
cloistered	jovial	sundry
dauntless	malevolence	tyrant
fruitless	pious	vile

Activity Option 1: Figurative Language
*Use characters and/or events from the play to form a sentence using each of your vocabulary words **figuratively**. Be sure to use any of the figures of speech— metaphor, simile, personification, hyperbole, etc. Once you have written your sentence, be sure to indicate which figure of speech you used to form your sentence.*

For example, if your vocabulary word was the word "ravenous," you might write:
1. *Vocabulary Word: ravenous*
   a. *Lady Macbeth's <u>ravenous</u> desire for power pushed Macbeth to embrace the dark side.*
   b. *metaphor*

Activity Option 2: Word Illustrations
Using 3 x 5 index cards, make a set of picture cards to help you learn your vocabulary words. Write the vocabulary words from Act Three on one side of the card, then illustrate or find a picture (if you download and print from online, be sure to cite your source!!) that helps you remember the definition of the word on the other side.

Activity Option 3: Word Analysis
Analyze each vocabulary word from Act Three. For each word:
   a. *Find the word in Act Three; then copy the line in which the word is found.*
   b. *Find 2-3 synonyms using a dictionary or thesaurus.*
   c. *Find 2-3 variations of the word using a dictionary or thesaurus.*

Macbeth
Act Four
Scene Guide

Scene One: The Witches' Cave	
Characters	
Action	
Staging	
Problem or Solution? How or Why?	
Scene Two: Macduff's Castle at Fife	
Characters	
Action	
Staging	
Problem or Solution? How or Why?	
Scene Three: England, King Edward's Court	
Characters	
Action	
Staging	
Problem or Solution? How or Why?	

Make a prediction about what you believe will happen in the last act of the play.

My prediction: _____

_____

Name _____ Period _____

Macbeth
Act Four
Comprehension Check

Directions: *To give you a comprehensive understanding of all aspects of the play, answer the following questions using complete sentences on a separate sheet of paper. Be sure to use your Scene Guide to help you.*

Scene One

1. What is the first apparition and what does it say?

2. What is the second apparition and what does it tell Macbeth? Why does Macbeth feel he can ignore the first apparition's warning?

3. What is the third apparition? What does it tell Macbeth? Why does Macbeth feel he can dismiss this apparition as well?

4. What final question does Macbeth have for the witches? What do the witches show him?

5. What is ironic about Macbeth's line "Infected be the air whereon they ride, / And damned all those that trust them"?

6. To where has Macduff fled? What is Macbeth's solution to this new problem?

Scene Two

1. What is Macduff's wife's reaction to the news that Macduff has left her?

2. How does Ross justify Macduff's actions to his wife?

3. What does Lady Macduff tell her son about Macduff?

4. What does Macduff's son say about Lady Macduff?

5. Why doesn't Lady Macduff leave after she has been warned?

Scene Three

1. Why doesn't Malcolm initially trust Macduff?

2. What do Malcolm and Macduff now call Macbeth? What do they think about how Macbeth has been running the country?

3. How does Malcolm "test" Macduff's allegiance?

4. What kinds of things does Malcolm say he would do as king? List two.

5. Who has Malcolm joined forces with? What have they already done to go against Macbeth?

6. Describe what Edward the Confessor, King of England, has done for his people, according to Malcolm.

7. What news does Ross bring Macduff? What is Macduff's immediate reaction? What does he then realize?

8. What does Macduff vow to do at the end of this scene?

Macbeth
Act Four
Standards Focus: Character Analysis

One of Shakespeare's talents is the ability to create powerful, realistic characters in his plays. By analyzing the interactions between characters and exploring how those interactions affect the plot, we can understand the play better, and therefore, grasp the themes or messages as Shakespeare intended.

For this activity, you will be completing an analysis of several characters in *Macbeth*. An explanation of some of the terms is below:

- **Main characters**: Main characters are those characters around which the plot revolves; generally, a character can be considered a main character when the story would be considerably different if the character were not a part of the story

- **Subordinate characters**: Subordinate characters are supporting characters. These characters are not really important to the plot of the story.

To help answer this section, ask yourself: *Does this character need to be in the story?* If *yes*, it is probably a main character. If *no*, it is probably a subordinate character.

- **Conflict**: a character or characters face a struggle or challenge
  - *Internal*: when a character faces a major decision or a physical or emotional struggle with his own morals, ethics, or conscience
  - *External*: when a character struggles against either another character, a force such as weather or nature, or some aspect of society

To help answer the *Internal Conflict* section, ask yourself: *What does this character wish to change about himself/herself?* Remember that this answer must be about some aspect of the character himself or herself, and not another character or outside force.
To help answer the *External Conflict* section, ask yourself: *What force does this character fight against the most?* This will be a person or some other outside force.

- **Motive**: in short, the reasons characters do what they do or make the choices they make

To help answer the section about *Motive*, ask yourself: *Why does the character feel they must take the action they take?* Motive is what a character wants or needs, while conflict is what ruins it (or tries to ruin it) for the character along the way.

- **Influences**: like people, characters can be influenced to behave a certain way. Characters can be influenced by another character, immediate situations, and background. While motive is the reason characters do what they do, a character's influences push the character either towards or away from his/her goals.

To help answer the section about *Influences*, ask yourself: *Besides the character himself or herself, who or what pushes the character to do what they do?*

Name _____ Period _____

Directions: *Now that you have read the majority of the play, complete the chart below, analyzing the main conflicts, motivations, and influences for each character to this point. The chart has been started for you—be sure to complete the chart that has been **started** for Macbeth before moving on to the others.*

Character	Macbeth
Main/ Subordinate	Main
Internal Conflict(s)	At first, Macbeth is willing to do anything for his country and his king. Then, after the witches' prophecies, he would do anything to become king. After he murders Duncan, he feels…
External Conflict(s)	Macbeth versus Duncan; Macbeth versus Banquo; Macbeth versus…
Main Motive	to be king of Scotland
Influence(s)	
Character	**Lady Macbeth**
Main/ Subordinate	
Internal Conflict(s)	
External Conflict(s)	
Main Motive	
Influence(s)	
Character	**Macduff**
Main/ Subordinate	
Internal Conflict(s)	
External Conflict(s)	
Main Motive	
Influence(s)	

Name _____ Period _____

Macbeth
Act Four
Standards Focus: Motif

A **motif** is a symbol that appears time and again over the course of a story, reinforcing the themes of a novel. A motif can be an action, symbol, place, statement, or even an object. Although a theme and a motif sound like the same thing, the main difference is that a motif is something that supports the theme. For example, if the theme of a novel is "the truth will eventually reveal itself," a motif from that novel might be two or three scenes that are set at night, behind which some sort of truth or secret is hidden, but is eventually revealed as day or light is seen.

Directions: *To help you learn how to find and understand motifs, complete the activity below. First, using Acts One through Four of the play, fill in three examples of the motif from the text (**be sure to include speaker, act, and scene**). Then, decide what theme the motifs the examples reveal. If you need more room, continue your answers on a separate sheet of paper.*

1. **Motif: Blood**

   a. Example: _____

   _____

   b. Example: _____

   _____

   c. Example: _____

   _____

   d. Significance/Meaning of Motif in the play: _____

   _____

   _____

2. **Motif: Sleep**

   a. Example: _____

   _____

   b. Example: _____

   _____

   c. Example: _____

   _____

   d. Significance/Meaning of Motif in the play: _____

   _____

   _____

Name _____ Period _____

3. **Motif: Reversal of Nature**

    a. Example: _____

    _____

    b. Example: _____

    _____

    c. Example: _____

    _____

    d. Significance/Meaning of Motif in the play: _____

    _____

    _____

4. **Motif: Visions/Hallucinations/Supernatural Elements**

    a. Example: _____

    _____

    b. Example: _____

    _____

    c. Example: _____

    _____

    d. Significance/Meaning of Motif in the play: _____

    _____

    _____

5. **Motif: Darkness and Night**

    a. Example: _____

    _____

    b. Example: _____

    _____

    c. Example: _____

    _____

    d. Significance/Meaning of Motif in the play: _____

    _____

    _____

Macbeth
Act Four
Assessment Preparation: Vocabulary Extension

Directions: *Using the vocabulary words from Act Four, answer the following questions. Write your answer on the line provided. Each word will be used only once.*

antic	avaricious	bodements	cistern	desolate
dolor	entrails	laudable	malady	pernicious
quarry	relish	resolute	sovereignty	teems

1. Which word best describes a desert landscape? _____

2. Since she was older by two years, Catherine felt she held _____ over her little sister and brother.

3. The gym _____ with students at every pep rally.

4. In Shakespeare's time, the Black plague could be described as a _____ malady.

5. This is a waterproof receptacle for storing water: _____

6. Someone who chooses to pursue something, regardless of the challenge or struggle could be considered _____ .

7. The tiger lost his _____ as it quickly climbed up a large tree.

8. This word describes what you might find after you hit a small animal with your car:

    _____

9. Dalilah ate her hot dog with mustard and relish with great _____ .

10. This word describes someone who should be commended for a good deed.

    _____

11. Mischievous children often engage in these which might get them into trouble:

    _____

12. When someone loses a loved one, they are very likely to be in a state of

    _____ .

13. Dark, thick clouds can be considered _____ of a pending storm.

14. In Shakespeare's day, even a minor _____ could cause death due to the lack of proper healthcare and medicines.

15. You should watch your wallet around someone who is _____ .

Name _____ Period _____

Macbeth
Act Five
Scene Guide

Scene One: Macbeth's Castle at Dunsinane	
Characters	
Action	
Staging	
Problem or Solution? How or Why?	
Scene Two: Outside Dunsinane	
Characters	
Action	
Staging	
Problem or Solution? How or Why?	
Scene Three: Inside Macbeth's Castle	
Characters	
Action	
Staging	
Problem or Solution? How or Why?	
Scene Four: Birnam Wood	
Characters	
Action	
Staging	
Problem or Solution? How or Why?	

Scene Five: Inside Macbeth's Castle	
Characters	
Action	
Staging	
Problem or Solution? How or Why?	

Scene Six: Outside Macbeth's Castle	
Characters	
Action	
Staging	
Problem or Solution? How or Why?	

Scene Seven: Inside Macbeth's Castle	
Characters	
Action	
Staging	
Problem or Solution? How or Why?	

Scene Eight: Outside Macbeth's Castle	
Characters	
Action	
Staging	
Problem or Solution? How or Why?	

Macbeth
Act Five
Comprehension Check

Directions: *To give you a comprehensive understanding of all aspects of the play, answer the following questions using complete sentences on a separate sheet of paper. Be sure to use your Scene Guide to help you.*

Scene One

1. Why is a doctor visiting the Macbeth household?

2. What strange behavior has Lady Macbeth been exhibiting? What does she say?

3. What does the Doctor say Lady Macbeth needs? What does he tell Lady Macbeth's gentlewoman to do for her?

Scene Two

1. Who has gathered to fight Macbeth? Where have they planned to meet?

2. What has Macbeth done in response to the insurgence?

Scene Three

1. What is Macbeth thinking about at the beginning of this scene? How does he try to convince himself that he should not be afraid?

2. What does the servant report to Macbeth?

3. What does Macbeth want Seyton to do for him?

4. What does Macbeth tell the Doctor to do for Lady Macbeth? What is the Doctor's reaction to Macbeth's request?

Scene Four

1. What orders does Malcolm give at Birnam? Why is this important?

Scene Five

1. What is Macbeth's reaction to the news of his wife's death?

2. In this scene, Macbeth speaks some of the most famous lines in Shakespeare: "Out, out brief candle! / Life's but a walking shadow, a poor player / That struts his hour upon the stage / And then is heard no more. It is a tale / Told by an idiot, full of sound and fury, / Signifying nothing." What does this quote mean and what does it reveal about Macbeth's feelings about life and death? Explain.

3. What news does the messenger bring to Macbeth? Why is this news unsettling to him?

Scene Six (none)

Scene Seven

1. Who does Macbeth kill and why does Macbeth feel he is now safe?

2. Who shows up looking for Macbeth?

Scene Eight

1. Why does Macbeth hesitate to kill Macduff?

2. What do we learn about Macduff?

3. How does Macbeth regain some sense of manhood in his last moments of life?

4. What news does Ross break to Old Siward?

5. What trophy does Macduff bring to the people of Scotland?

6. Who becomes King? Why is this ending surprising, considering the witches' predictions?

7. Were the witches' predictions real? Believable? Are the witches to blame for Macbeth's eventual death? Why or why not? Explain your thoughts on the predictions, Macbeth's actions, and ending of the story.

Macbeth
Act Five
Standards Focus: Tragedy and the Tragic Hero

Over 2,300 years ago, the Greek philosopher Aristotle wrote his definition of a **tragedy**. According to Aristotle: "Tragedy, then, is an imitation of an action that is serious, complete, and of a certain magnitude; with incidents arousing pity and fear, wherewith to accomplish its catharsis of such emotions." In other words, to be a true tragedy, a story must make the audience pity the characters and make them fear the same consequences the character (usually the protagonist) experiences.

Similarly, Aristotle defined the concept of a tragic hero. A **tragic hero** is a protagonist with a fatal (also called tragic) flaw that eventually leads to his downfall. The Aristotelian tragic hero is introduced as happy, powerful, and privileged, and ends up dying or suffering immensely because of his own actions or mistakes. The tragic hero must have four characteristics: goodness (a moral and ethical person), superiority (such as someone with supreme or noble authority or control), a tragic flaw—called *hamartia*—which will eventually lead him to his own demise, and the eventual realization that his decisions or actions have caused his downfall (faces death or suffering with honor). Usually, the realization of tragic flaw results in an **epiphany**, or a sudden realization by the character, audience, or both, and a **catharsis**, or a release of emotions, which makes the audience feel more at peace with their own lives.

Directions: *Many scholars debate whether Macbeth is a true tragic hero. Analyze the character of Macbeth and the play as a whole by answering the questions below.*

1. In your opinion, does Macbeth have a tragic flaw? If so, what is it?

2. When Macbeth is first introduced, is he happy? Why or why not?

3. How might Macbeth be considered a superior or privileged person?

4. In your opinion, is Macbeth a moral and/or ethical person?

5. At what point does Macbeth realize he is facing his own demise? What is his reaction? How is/isn't this consistent with the characteristics of the tragic hero?

6. Do you feel Macbeth is the ideal tragic hero? Why or why not? Explain how he fits or does not fit the definition of a tragic hero. What "rules" Macbeth—external forces or his own inner motivation? Explain.

7. According to the definition, is *Macbeth* a tragedy? Why or why not? Support your response with evidence from the play. Do you feel pity for the characters, especially Macbeth? Did you experience a catharsis, or emotional release, because you did not suffer the same fate as Macbeth? Why or why not?

Name _____ Period _____

Macbeth
Act Five
Standards Focus: Theme

Theme is the central idea or message in a work of literature. Theme should not be confused with the subject of the work, but rather, theme is a general statement about life or human nature. Shakespeare is known for telling stories with universal themes, or ideas to which people across time and cultures can relate. *Macbeth* has several themes, and the reader or audience must take a good look at the entire play (the title, plot, characters, setting, and mood) which all work together to reveal the themes.

Part One
Directions*: Complete the following chart, finding an example from throughout the play that exemplifies and illustrates each theme. Be sure to write down the direct quote, including the speaker, the situation, and where the example is found (Act, Scene, Line[s]). Finally, explain how this particular quote illustrates the theme.*

1. *Theme:* **Ambition**

    a. Quote/Speaker: _____

    _____

    _____

    b. Situation: _____

    _____

    _____

    c. Act, Scene, Line(s): _____

    d. Explanation: _____

    _____

    _____

2. *Theme:* **Guilt**

    a. Quote/Speaker: _____

    _____

    b. Situation: _____

    _____

    _____

    c. Act, Scene, Line(s): _____

    d. Explanation: _____

    _____

    _____

Name _____ Period _____

3. *Theme:* **Trust versus Betrayal**

    a. Quote/Speaker: _____

    _____

    _____

    b. Situation: _____

    _____

    _____

    c. Act, Scene, Line(s): _____

    d. Explanation: _____

    _____

    _____

4. *Theme:* **Fate versus Free Will**

    a. Quote/Speaker: _____

    _____

    _____

    b. Situation: _____

    _____

    _____

    c. Act, Scene, Line(s): _____

    d. Explanation: _____

    _____

    _____

5. *Theme:* **Nature versus the Unnatural**

    a. Quote/Speaker: _____

    _____

    _____

    b. Situation: _____

    _____

    _____

    c. Act, Scene, Line(s): _____

    d. Explanation: _____

    _____

Name _____ Period _____

Part Two

Directions: *Answer the following questions using complete sentences. Be sure to use examples from the text to support your response.*

1. One of the themes of *Macbeth* is: *Unchecked power can lead to corruption.* Outside of the story of *Macbeth*, what other works of literature have this theme? What kind of real life examples can you find of this? Explain.

_____

_____

_____

_____

_____

_____

_____

2. Another theme that permeates the play is: *The power of suggestion can drown one's conscience.* Do you agree or disagree with this statement? Why? Give an example from your own life in which this statement is true. Explain.

_____

_____

_____

_____

_____

_____

3. Why is it important for an author to present theme(s) in a work of literature?

_____

_____

_____

4. What do you feel is the most important theme of Macbeth? Explain.

_____

_____

_____

_____

Name _____ Period _____

Macbeth
Act Five
Assessment Preparation: Vocabulary in Context

Directions: *For this exercise, answer each question or statement using <u>as much detail as possible</u>. Note: vocabulary words may appear in a different part of speech in the question or statement. An example has been done for you.*

Ex. If someone is being **aloof** with you, how might they behave?

If someone is being aloof, they might avoid eye contact, look away often, turn their back, or stand far away.

1. When someone tries to **arbitrate** an argument, what actions might he/she take?

   _____

   _____

2. What kinds of things **perturb** you? _____

   _____

   _____

3. If you are being **upbraided**, what is happening to you? _____

   _____

   _____

4. What was the traitor, Thane of Cawdor, condemned to? _____

   _____

   _____

5. What caused **fury** in Macbeth? _____

   _____

   _____

6. If an antique were in **pristine** condition, would it be worth more or less? Why?

   _____

   _____

   _____

7. If you were building a model house out of toothpicks, why would you want to **fortify** it? _____

   _____

_____

_____

8. If you were living a **divinely** inspired life, what might life be like for you? ____

_____

_____

_____

9. Why do you think teenagers tend to **revolt** against their parents? _____

_____

_____

_____

10. If your reputation is **marred** somehow, what may have happened? _____

_____

_____

_____

11. If a little brother were **pestering** you, how would you deal with it? _____

_____

_____

12. If a snake suddenly **recoils**, what might it be about to do? _____

_____

_____

13. What kinds of people can be considered the modern **gentry** in the U.S.? _____

_____

_____

14. What happens if you **agitate** a soda can before opening it? _____

_____

_____

15. What aspects of a swamp contribute to its **murkiness**? _____

_____

_____

Name _____ Period _____

Macbeth
Act One Quiz

Part A: Character Matching
***Directions**: Match the characters on the left with the description or action on the right. Write the letter of the correct answer on the line provided.*

1. _____ Macbeth
2. _____ Lady Macbeth
3. _____ Banquo
4. _____ Malcolm
5. _____ Macdonwald
6. _____ Duncan
7. _____ three Witches
8. _____ Thane of Cawdor

a. will never be king, but will be the father of kings
b. comes up with the plan to assassinate the king
c. Duncan's eldest son
d. executed for being a traitor
e. "Hover through the fog and filthy air"
f. head was cut off and placed on a sword
g. King of Scotland
h. If chance wants him to be king "chance will crown" him

Part B: True/False
***Directions**: Read each statement carefully. If the statement is false, write the word "false" on the line. If the statement is true, write the word "true" on the line.*

9. _____ The witches plan to meet Macbeth on a hill before the war.

10. _____ Lady Macbeth has doubts about whether they should kill the king.

11. _____ The war was between Scotland and Sweden.

12. _____ Lady Macbeth said "Take my milk for gall, you murd'ring ministers"

13. _____ Macbeth initially had doubts about the witches' prophecies.

Part C: Multiple Choice
***Directions**: Write the letter of the best choice on the line provided.*

14. _____ What does "False face must hide what the false heart doth know" mean?
   a. Your feelings are false.
   b. You must act out your revenge.
   c. You do not know how to behave.
   d. You must hide your true feelings.

15. _____ Lady Macbeth's plan is to blame the murder on:
   a. Duncan's guards
   b. the witches
   c. Banquo
   d. Malcolm

16. _____ Why did the witches harm the fat lady's husband?
   a. She wouldn't give them money.
   b. She wouldn't share her chestnuts.
   c. She lied to them.
   d. She told the witches that she didn't believe their prophecies.

17. _____ How does Lady Macbeth react when Macbeth calls off the plan?
   a. She is confused.
   b. She is disappointed.
   c. She is furious.
   d. She is understanding.

18. _____ Why is Banquo confused by the witches?
   a. He can't understand what they are saying.
   b. He thinks they are women, but they have beards.
   c. He doesn't believe they can tell the future.
   d. He thinks they are men, but they speak like women.

Part D: Quote Matching

Directions: *Match the quote on the right with the speaker on the left. Write the letter of the correct answer on the line provided.*

19. _____ Macbeth

20. _____ King Duncan

21. _____ Lady Macbeth

22. _____ Banquo

23. _____ Captain

24. _____ Witch

25. _____ Malcolm

   a. *For brave Macbeth—well he deserves that name—/ Disdaining Fortune, with his brandished steel, / Which smoked with bloody execution, Like valor's minion carved out his bloody passage / Till he faced the slave*

   b. *My noble partner / You greet with present grace and great prediction / Of noble having and of royal hope, / That he seems rapt withal. To me you speak not.*

   c. *O worthiest cousin, / The sin of my ingratitude even now / Was heavy on me.*

   d. *Come, you spirits / That tend on mortal thoughts, unsex me here, / And fill me from the crown to the topful / Of direst cruelty.*

   e. *When the hurly-burly's done, / When the battle's lost and won.*

   f. *Two truths are told, / As happy prologues to the swelling act of the imperial theme.*

   g. *I have spoke / With one that saw him die, who did report / That very frankly he confessed his treasons, / Implored your highness's pardon and set forth / A deep repentance.*

Part E. Short Response

Directions: *Answer the following questions on a separate piece of paper, and then attach your answers to your quiz. Be sure to use as many details as possible in your response in order to answer the question fully.*

26. How did Macbeth earn the respect of the King?

27. Summarize the witches' prophecies for both Macbeth and Banquo.

28. Explain what Lady Macbeth asks the spirits to do to her to get her "ready" for the King's execution.

Name _____ Period _____

Macbeth
Act One Vocabulary Quiz

Directions: *Match each vocabulary word with the correct definition or synonym. Write the letter of the answer on the line provided next to the vocabulary word.*

_____ 1. chalice

_____ 2. chastise

_____ 3. compunctious

_____ 4. dwindle

_____ 5. harbinger

_____ 6. implored

_____ 7. ingratitude

_____ 8. interim

_____ 9. mettle

_____ 10. minion

_____ 11. plight

_____ 12. prophetic

_____ 13. surmise

_____ 14. trifles

_____ 15. withered

a. 1) involved by logical necessity; entail; 2) appealed to; beseeched

b. a cup or goblet

c. a period between two events

d. deserving of shame; deeply wrong

e. difficult or adverse situation

f. dried up or shriveled, as if from a loss of moisture

g. lack of gratitude; ungratefulness

h. of, or a characteristic of, a prophet or prophecy

i. one that indicates or foreshadows what is to come; forerunner

j. strength of character; determination

k. submissive follower or dependent

l. things of little importance or value; small amounts

m. 1) to infer with little evidence; guess; 2) an idea or opinion based on little evidence; conjecture

n. to make or become gradually less until little remains

o. to punish by beating; to criticize severely

Name _____ Period _____

Macbeth
Act Two Quiz

Part A: Character Matching
Directions: *Match the characters on the left with the description, quote, or action on the right. Write the letter of the correct answer on the line provided.*

1. _____ Banquo

2. _____ Fleance

3. _____ Macbeth

4. _____ Lady Macbeth

5. _____ Porter

6. _____ Macduff

7. _____ Lennox

8. _____ Malcolm

9. _____ Donalbain

10. _____ Ross

a. "But this place is too cold for hell."

b. imagines a dagger leading him to the king's chamber

c. Banquo's son

d. "Give me the daggers. The sleeping and the dead are but pictures."

e. found the king dead

f. sees the "daggers in men's smiles"

g. saw the king's horses eat each other

h. arrives with Macduff to wake the king

i. has nightmares about the witches

j. flees to England

Part B: True/False
Directions: *Read each statement carefully. If the statement is false, write the word "false" on the line. If the statement is true, write the word "true" on the line.*

11. _____ The weather and environment are indicators of strange happenings in this act.

12. _____ Macbeth does not have any second thoughts about killing King Duncan, since the witches said it must happen.

13. _____ Macbeth lies to Banquo, stating that he never thinks of the witches.

14. _____ Macbeth is afraid of what will happen to him, since he is unable to say "amen."

15. _____ Lady Macbeth could not murder the king herself because Duncan looked too much like her father.

16. _____ Lady Macbeth murders Duncan's guards when she feels Macbeth has failed.

17. _____ Lady Macbeth is upset that there is so much blood involved in killing Duncan.

Name _____ Period _____

18. _____ Macbeth gets drunk in this act.

19. _____ The Porter is meant to provide comic relief.

20. _____ The men understand and appreciate Macbeth killing Duncan's
guards.

Part C: Quote Matching
Directions: Match the quote on the right with the speaker on the left. Write the letter of the correct answer on the line provided.

21. _____ Macbeth

22. _____ Lady Macbeth

23. _____ Ross

24. _____ Malcolm

25. _____ Macduff

26. _____ Lennox

27. _____ Porter

a. *A little water clears us of this deed. / How easy is it then!*

b. *By th' clock 'tis day, / And yet dark night strangles the travelling lamp.*

c. *He did command me to call timely on him; / I have almost slipped the hour.*

d. *Hear it not, Duncan, for it is a knell / That summons thee to heaven, or to hell.*

e. *O come in, equivocator. Knock, knock, knock.*

f. *The obscure bird / Clamored the livelong night. Some say the earth / Was feverous and did shake.*

g. *Therefore to horse, / And let us not be dainty of leave-taking / But shift away.*

Part D. Short Response
Directions: Answer the following questions on a separate piece of paper, and then attach your answers to your quiz. Be sure to use as many details as possible in your response in order to answer the question fully.

28. Explain the content and purpose of the Porter and his speech in this act.

29. Explain the significance of both Macbeth and Lady Macbeth getting blood on their hands. How does each of them react to the blood? What does this reveal about their characters and their intentions?

30. Explain the significance of the "unnatural acts" that have pervaded this act. Name three of these acts and explain their symbolism.

Macbeth
Act Two Vocabulary Quiz

Directions: *Match each vocabulary word with the correct definition or synonym. Write the letter of the answer on the line provided next to the vocabulary word.*

_____ 1. allegiance

_____ 2. augment

_____ 3. carousing

_____ 4. clamored

_____ 5. dire

_____ 6. gild

_____ 7. lamentings

_____ 8. malice

_____ 9. palpable

_____ 10. parley

_____ 11. predominance

_____ 12. provoke

_____ 13. quenched

_____ 14. scruples

_____ 15. summons

a. a severe, serious, or desperate situation or circumstance

b. able to be felt, touched

c. appearing as most important, powerful; strongest or most common in number or amount

d. calling for service or action

e. drinking and becoming noisy

f. expressions of grief or sorrow

g. intention or desire to cause great harm to someone

h. loyalty to a ruler or country

i. moral or ethical considerations

j. satisfied thirst or desire

k. shouted and demanded noisily

l. to add something in order to make it larger or more substantial

m. to cover with a substance, usually gold or gold-like

n. to stir emotion in someone; arouse

o. to talk or negotiate; speak with

Macbeth
Act Three Quiz

Part A: Character Matching
Directions: *Match the characters on the left with the description or action on the right. Write the letter of the correct answer on the line provided.*

1. _____ Banquo

2. _____ Fleance

3. _____ Macbeth

4. _____ Lady Macbeth

5. _____ Hecate

6. _____ Macduff

7. _____ Lennox

8. _____ Malcolm

a. "Be innocent of the knowledge, dearest chuck / Till thou applaud the deed."

b. suspects Macbeth of Banquo's murder

c. "Naught's had, all's spent, / Where our desire is got without content."

d. angry she was not consulted in Macbeth's affairs and to be able to show her "art"

e. safely escapes the ambush

f. suspects Macbeth of murdering Duncan

g. refused Macbeth's summons

h. safely living in England with King Edward

Part B: True/False

Directions: *Read each statement carefully. If the statement is false, write the word "false" on the line. If the statement is true, write the word "true" on the line.*

9. _____ Two murderers ambushed Banquo.

10. _____ Macbeth startles his dinner guests by suffering from an epileptic seizure.

11. _____ Macbeth sees the ghost of Duncan at the table.

12. _____ Lady Macbeth sees the ghost.

13. _____ Lady Macbeth tells Macbeth that he needs some sleep.

14. _____ The goddess of witchcraft is named Hecate.

15. _____ Lady Macbeth is beginning to regret how she became queen.

16. _____ Banquo secretly hopes that the witches' prophecies will come true for him, too.

17. _____ Macbeth is okay with not having his sons take over the throne, as long as he is able to be king.

18. _____ Macbeth tells the murderers that he would kill Banquo himself, but it wouldn't "look good" to others if he did.

Name _____ Period _____

Part C: Quote Response

Directions: For each of the following excerpts from Act Three: a) identify the speaker, b) explain the situation (what is happening) and c) give the importance of the quote to the play so far.

19. *Our fears in Banquo stick deep, / And in his royalty of nature reigns that which would be feared.*

    a. Speaker:_____

    b. Situation: _____

    _____

    c. Importance: _____

    _____

20. *Thou hast it now: King, Cawdor, Glamis, all / As the weird women promised, and I fear / Thou play'dst most foully for 't.*

    a. Speaker:_____

    b. Situation: _____

    _____

    c. Importance: _____

    _____

21. *Sit worthy friends. My lord is often thus, / And hath been from his youth. Pray you, keep seat. / The fit is momentary; upon a thought / He will again be well.*

    a. Speaker:_____

    b. Situation: _____

    _____

    c. Importance: _____

    _____

22. *Nought's had, all's spent, / Where our desire is got without content. / 'Tis safer to be that which we destroy / Than by destruction dwell in doubtful joy.*

    a. Speaker:_____

    b. Situation: _____

    _____

    c. Importance: _____

    _____

Part D. Short Response

Directions: Answer the following questions on a separate piece of paper, and then attach your answers to your quiz. Be sure to use as many details as possible in your response in order to answer the question fully.

23. Summarize the events and purpose of Act Three, Scene 5—the witches' scene.

24. Identify how we see Macbeth's support waning in this act. What hints or clues are we given that Macbeth's reign will soon be challenged?

25. Explain the dramatic change in Macbeth since the beginning of the play. Be sure to include details about the differences in the murders of Duncan and Banquo, the appearance of the ghost, as well as his relationship with Lady Macbeth.

Name _____ Period _____

Macbeth
Act Three Vocabulary Quiz

Directions: *Match each vocabulary word with the correct definition or synonym. Write the letter of the answer on the line provided next to the vocabulary word.*

_____ 1.   affliction

_____ 2.   chide

_____ 3.   cloistered

_____ 4.   dauntless

_____ 5.   fruitless

_____ 6.   grapple

_____ 7.   incensed

_____ 8.   jovial

_____ 9.   malevolence

_____ 10. pious

_____ 11. purged

_____ 12. scepter

_____ 13. sundry

_____ 14. tyrant

_____ 15. vile

a. a condition of great physical or mental distress

b. a harsh or cruel leader

c. cheerful; happy

d. fearless; unable to be intimidated

e. made extremely angry

f. religious; devout

g. secluded from the world

h. unproductive or unsuccessful

i. disgusting; wicked; unpleasant

j. a ceremonial staff or rod

k. great evil or harm

l. to put down; to tell someone off

m. removed something undesirable or imperfect

n. wrestle or struggle with

o. various; miscellaneous

Name _____ Period _____

Macbeth
Act Four Quiz

Part A: Character Matching
Directions: *Match the characters on the left with the description or action on the right. Write the letter of the correct answer on the line provided.*

1. _____ the armed head
2. _____ the bloody child
3. _____ the crowned child
4. _____ Lennox
5. _____ Macbeth
6. _____ Macduff
7. _____ Ross
8. _____ Lady Macduff
9. _____ Macduff's son
10. _____ Malcolm

a. "beware Macduff."

b. "none of woman born shall harm Macbeth"

c. a "prattler" beyond his years

d. calls Macduff a traitor

e. delivers the bad news to Macduff

f. entire family is slaughtered

g. Macbeth cannot be harmed "until Great Birnam wood to high Dunsinane hill / Shall come against him"

h. notifies Macbeth that Macduff is gone to England

i. tests Macduff to see where his allegiance lies

j. wants to know if Banquo's descendants will reign

Part B: True/False
Directions: *Read each statement carefully. If the statement is false, write the word "false" on the line. If the statement is true, write the word "true" on the line.*

11. _____ Macbeth is confident about his future.

12. _____ Macduff is a coward who abandoned his family.

13. _____ The witches warn Macbeth about Lady Macbeth.

14. _____ Lady Macduff understands and graciously accepts why her husband left.

15. _____ Malcolm and Macduff join forces to overthrow Macbeth.

16. _____ Ross vows revenge against Macbeth.

17. _____ Macduff's son is the only one who survives.

18. _____ The witches showed Macbeth a line of men who looked like Banquo.

Part C: Quote Matching
Directions: *Match the quote on the left with the speaker on the right. Write the letter of the correct answer on the line provided.*

19. _____ *Nay, how will you do for a husband?*

20. _____ *Infected be the air upon which they ride; / And damn'd all those that trust them!*

21. _____ *All my pretty ones? Did you say all? O Hell-kite – All?*

22. _____ *When our actions do not, our fears do make us traitors.*

23. _____ *Your wives, your daughters, / Your matrons, and your maids could not fill up / The cistern of my lust, and my desire / All continent impediments would o'erbear / That did oppose my will.*

a. Macbeth
b. Macduff's son
c. Macduff
d. Malcolm
e. Lady Macduff

Part D. Short Response
Directions: *Answer the following questions on the lines below. Be sure to use as many details as possible in your response in order to answer the question fully. Use a separate piece of paper and attach it to this quiz if you need more room to answer.*

24. Which apparition angers Macbeth? Why does it anger him? How do the apparitions confuse Macbeth, as Hecate promised?

_____

_____

_____

_____

_____

25. The conversation between Lady Macduff and her son seems out of place in this play. What might be the explanation of this scene? What is your impression of Lady Macduff and her relationship with Macduff, based upon this scene?

_____

_____

_____

_____

_____

Name _____ Period _____

Macbeth
Act Four Vocabulary Quiz

Directions: *Match each vocabulary word with the correct definition or synonym. Write the letter of the answer on the line provided next to the vocabulary word.*

_____ 1. dolor

_____ 2. entrails

_____ 3. laudable

_____ 4. sovereignty

_____ 5. teems

_____ 6. antic

_____ 7. avaricious

_____ 8. bodements

_____ 9. malady

_____ 10. pernicious

_____ 11. quarry

_____ 12. relish

_____ 13. resolute

_____ 14. cistern

_____ 15. desolate

a. has an extremely large number or amount; overflows

b. deadly or destructive

c. having extreme desire for wealth; greedy

d. having, or motivated by, determination

e. praiseworthy; commendable

f. without inhabitants; deserted

g. intense sadness

h. a childish act or gesture

i. a physical or psychological disorder or disease

j. a tank for storing water

k. an animal or bird that is hunted

l. internal organs, especially the intestines

m. omens; foreshadowing

n. supreme authority or rule

o. to enjoy or take pleasure in something

Name _____ Period _____

Macbeth
Act Five Quiz

Part A: Character Matching
Directions: *Match the characters on the left with the description or action on the right. Write the letter of the correct answer on the line provided.*

1. _____ Macbeth

2. _____ Lady Macbeth

3. _____ Macduff

4. _____ Seyton

5. _____ Lady Macbeth's attendant

6. _____ Angus

a. "Out, damned spot! out, I say! – One, two. Why, then, 'tis time to do' t. Hell is murky!"

b. wants the Doctor to just give Lady Macbeth some medicine to "cure" her ills

c. has heard Lady Macbeth confess to the murders

d. Macbeth's servant

e. "Now does he feel his title / Hang loose about him, like a giant's robe / Upon a dwarfish thief."

f. "Tyrant, show thy face! / If thou be'st slain and with no stroke of mine, / My wife and children's ghosts will haunt me still."

Part B: True/False
Directions: *Read each statement carefully. If the statement is false, write the word "false" on the line. If the statement is true, write the word "true" on the line.*

7. _____ Lady Macbeth's doctor knows he cannot cure her, and fears she may kill herself.

8. _____ Malcolm, Siward, and Macduff have joined forces to overthrow Macbeth.

9. _____ Macbeth does not fear Malcolm because he is "of woman born."

10. _____ The doctor watches Lady Macbeth attempt to cut herself.

11. _____ Macbeth's fears are temporarily set aside when he kills young Siward.

12. _____ Macbeth hesitates to kill Macduff because he feels guilty about killing Macduff's family.

13. _____ Macduff becomes the new King of Scotland.

14. _____ Lady Macbeth talks to herself and Macbeth when she sleepwalks.

15. _____ Macbeth kills Lady Macbeth to relieve her of her sickness.

16. _____ Lady Macbeth insists she have someone beside her at all times.

17. _____ Malcolm cuts off Macbeth's head as a trophy of battle.

Part C: Quote Matching
Directions: *Match the quote on the right with the speaker on the left. Write the letter of the correct answer on the line provided.*

18. _____ *The devil himself could not pronounce / a title more hateful to mine ear.*

19. _____ *I have no words. My voice is in my sword. / Thou bloodier villain than terms can give thee out!*

20. _____ *Seyton! —I am sick at heart, / When I behold— Seyton, I say!"*

21. _____ *She has spoke what she should not, I am sure of that. Heaven knows what she has known.*

22. _____ *The Queen, my lord, is dead.*

23. _____ *The Thane of Fife had a wife: where is she now? / What, will these hands ne'er be clean?*

a. Macbeth
b. Lady Macbeth
c. Seyton
d. Lady Macbeth's attendant
e. Macduff
f. Young Siward

Part D. Short Response
Directions: *Answer the following questions on the lines below. Be sure to use as many details as possible in your response in order to answer the question fully. Use a separate piece of paper and attach it to this quiz if you need more room to answer.*

24. Explain how the prophecies "Birnam Wood comes to Dunsinane" and "none of woman born shall harm Macbeth" come true. _____

_____

_____

_____

_____

25. Explain the meaning and significance of Macbeth's "Tomorrow" soliloquy in terms of the theme of the play and the universality of the message to you in your own life. _____

_____

_____

_____

_____

_____

_____

Name _____ Period _____

Macbeth
Act Five Vocabulary Quiz

Directions: *Match each vocabulary word with the correct definition or synonym. Write the letter of the answer on the line provided next to the vocabulary word.*

_____ 1. agitation   a. something that disturbs or makes one anxious

_____ 2. arbitrate   b. annoyed constantly; bothered

_____ 3. condemn   c. violent shaking or stirring; disturbance

_____ 4. divine   d. thick, gloomy, and hard to see through

_____ 5. fortifies   e. to judge or settle a dispute

_____ 6. fury   f. to consider a person guilty

_____ 7. gentry   g. rebellions against authority

_____ 8. mar   h. to damage or spoil

_____ 9. murky   i. connecting or relating to God or gods

_____ 10. perturbation   j. makes stronger

_____ 11. pestered   k. move back suddenly

_____ 12. pristine   l. remaining in a pure state; uncorrupted

_____ 13. recoil   m. to criticize sharply; to reprimand

_____ 14. revolts   n. uncontrollable anger or rage

_____ 15. upbraid   o. people of good family or high social position

Name _____ Period _____

Macbeth
Just for Fun! Crossword Puzzle

ACROSS

5 Birnam Wood comes to _____

9 This is the first title Macbeth inherits (Thane of _____)

12 "More is thy due than more than all can pay"

13 According to Macbeth, life is a tale told by an _____

14 The goddess of witchcraft

15 "Hear it not, Duncan, for it is a knell / That summons thee to heaven, or to hell."

18 Macbeth sees the ghost of _____ at the table.

19 Macbeth envisions this leading him towards Duncan's chamber.

20 Where Duncan is killed

24 Narrowly escapes being murdered

25 "All my pretty ones? Did you say all? O hell-kite!"

29 Tells Macduff that his family was killed

31 Lady Macbeth tries to _____ her hands when she is sleepwalking.

32 In Act One, Macbeth is afraid of what will happen to him, since he is unable to say "_____."

33 Macbeth's fears are temporarily set aside when he kills young _____.

34 "O come in, equivocator. Knock, knock, knock."

DOWN

1 Malcolm, _____, and Macduff joined forces to overthrow Macbeth.

2 "When the hurly-burly's done, / When the battle's lost and won."

3 Discovers Duncan's body

4 In Act Five, Lady Macbeth commanded she have this beside her at all times.

6 Flees Scotland to Ireland to avoid harm

7 "Out, out brief candle!"

8 "A little water clears us of this deed. / How easy is it then!"

10 Lady Macbeth talks to herself and Macbeth when she _____.

11 The three witches meet upon the _____

16 "Lechery, sir, it provokes and unprovokes."

17 Will never be king, but will be the father of kings

21 "Out damned _____ Out I say!"

22 This country invades Scotland at the end of the play

23 Scotland is at war with this country at the beginning of the play

25 Duncan's eldest son

26 The Porter is meant to provide _____ relief.

27 Lady Macbeth could not murder the king herself because Duncan looked too much like her _____

28 Mad she was not consulted in Macbeth's affairs to be able to show her "art"

30 Where kings are coronated in Scotland.

Name _____ Period _____

Macbeth
Final Test

Part A: Characters
Directions*: Match the following characters with the BEST description. Write the letter of the correct answer on the line provided. Answers will be used only once.*

1. _____ Duncan's youngest son; flees to Ireland

2. _____ "[Life] is a tale / Told by an idiot, full of sound and fury / Signifying nothing"

3. _____ jokes that he is Hell's gatekeeper

4. _____ goddess of witchcraft

5. _____ narrowly escapes being murdered

6. _____ far too trusting of others

7. _____ accuses her husband of being a traitor

8. _____ Duncan's named heir

9. _____ will never be king, but will be the father of kings

10. _____ becomes highly suspicious of Macbeth by Act Three

11. _____ hover through the "fog and filthy air"

12. _____ informs Macduff that his family was murdered

13. _____ "Out, damned spot! out, I say! – One, two. Why, then, 'tis time to do 't. Hell is murky!"

14. _____ Macbeth's servant, and the one he calls upon in his time of need

15. _____ "Tyrant, show thy face! / If thou be'st slain and with no stroke of mine, / My wife and children's ghosts will haunt me still."

a. Macbeth
b. Lady Macbeth
c. Macduff
d. Banquo
e. Duncan
f. Malcolm
g. Donalbain
h. Hecate
i. Porter
j. Ross
k. Fleance
l. Lennox
m. the Three Witches
n. Lady Macduff
o. Seyton

Part B: Multiple Choice: Reading
Directions*: Write the letter of the BEST answer on the line provided.*

16. _____ What does "False face must hide what the false heart doth know" mean?
   a. Your feelings are false.
   b. You must act out your revenge.
   c. You do not know how to behave.
   d. You must hide your true feelings.

17. _____ Lady Macbeth's plan is to blame Duncan's murder on:
   a. Duncan's guards
   b. the witches
   c. Banquo
   d. Malcolm

18. _____ Why did the witches harm the fat lady's husband?
   a. She wouldn't give them money.
   b. She wouldn't share her chestnuts.
   c. She lied to them.
   d. She told the witches that she didn't believe their prophecies.

19. _____ At the beginning of the play, the war was between:
    a. Scotland and Sweden   c. England and Scotland
    b. Scotland and Norway   d. England and Norway

20. _____ Which character provides comic relief in the play?
    a. Ross   c. Lennox
    b. Lady Macbeth   d. the Porter

21. _____ Which of the following was NOT a prediction given by the apparitions?
    a. "Beware Macduff"   c. Macbeth will never be harmed until
    b. "None of woman born shall harm   Birnam Wood comes to Dunsinane
       Macbeth"   d. "Thou shall get kings, though thou be none"

22. _____ Who joins Malcolm and Macduff to overthrow Macbeth at the end of the play?
    a. Fleance   c. Duncan
    b. Banquo   d. Siward

23. _____ Where is Duncan killed?
    a. Scone   c. Dunsinane
    b. Inverness   d. Birnam Wood

24. _____ Who discovers Duncan's body?
    a. Macbeth   c. Siward
    b. Macduff   d. the Porter

25. _____ What does Lady Macduff call her husband?
    a. villain   c. traitor
    b. hero   d. thief

26. _____ Who becomes King of Scotland at the end of the play?
    a. Macduff   c. Fleance
    b. Malcolm   d. Old Siward

27. _____ Who was "from his mother's womb, untimely ripped"?
    a. Macduff   c. Fleance
    b. Malcolm   d. Young Siward

28. _____ Macbeth sees all of the following apparitions EXCEPT:
    a. a line of men with mirrors   c. a child holding a burning cross
    b. a crowned child with a tree   d. a head with a helmet

29. _____ What is the prophecy given to Banquo?
    a. He will be the father of kings   c. He will become king
    b. He will be killed by someone close to   d. He will be labeled a traitor
       him

30. _____ Lady Macbeth can best be described as:
    a. loving and supportive   c. motherly and driven
    b. vengeful and sympathetic   d. ambitious and motivated

Name _____ Period _____

Part C: Quotes
Directions: *Using the box below, choose the name of the speaker of each of the following quotes. Write the speaker's name on the line provided.* **Note: Answers may be used more than once, and not all answers will be used.**

Macbeth	Lady Macbeth	Macduff
Duncan	the Porter	Banquo
the Captain	the Witches	Young Siward
Young Macduff	the Doctor	Lady Macbeth's attendant
Lady Macduff	Malcolm	Lennox

_____ 31. *A little water clears us of this deed. / How easy is it then!*

_____ 32. *I grant him bloody, / Luxurious, avaricious, false, deceitful, / Sudden, malicious, smacking of every sin / That has a name.*

_____ 33. *Fathered he is, and yet he's fatherless.*

_____ 34. *He did command me to call timely on him; / I have almost slipped the hour.*

_____ 35. *Damned fact! How it did grieve Macbeth!*

_____ 36. *The devil himself could not pronounce a title / More hateful to mine ear.*

_____ 37. *O come in, equivocator. Knock, knock, knock.*

_____ 38. *For brave Macbeth—well he deserves that name— / Disdaining Fortune, with his brandished steel, / Which smoked with bloody execution, Like valor's minion carved out his bloody passage / Till he faced the slave*

_____ 39. *My noble partner / You greet with present grace and great prediction / Of noble having and of royal hope, / That he seems rapt withal. To me you speak not.*

_____ 40. *Nay, how will you do for a husband?*

_____ 41. *Fair is foul and foul is fair.*

_____ 42. *Come, you spirits / That tend on mortal thoughts, unsex me here, / And fill me from the crown to the topful / Of direst cruelty.*

_____ 43. *Thou hast it now: King, Cawdor, Glamis, all / As the weird women promised, and I fear / Thou play'dst most foully for 't.*

_____ 44. *Foul whisp'rings are abroad. Unnatural deeds / Do breed unnatural troubles. Infected minds / To their deaf pillows will discharge their secrets.*

_____ 45. *She has spoke what she should not, I am sure of that. Heaven knows what she has known.*

_____ 46. *The Queen, my lord, is dead.*

Name _____ Period _____

Part D: Short Response (Numbers 47-50)

Directions: *Answer FOUR of the following short response questions on a separate piece of paper. Responses should be at least 4-6 thoughtful sentences, using details from the story as much as possible to support your response.*

- How did Macbeth earn the respect of the King in Act One?

- Summarize the witches' prophecies for both Macbeth and Banquo.

- Explain what Lady Macbeth asks the spirits to do to her to get her "ready" for the King's execution. Give as many details as possible.

- Explain the content and purpose of the Porter and his speech in Act Two.

- Explain the significance of both Macbeth and Lady Macbeth getting blood on their hands in Act Two. How does each of them react to the blood? What does this reveal about their characters and their intentions?

- Explain the meaning and significance of Macbeth's "Tomorrow" soliloquy (Act Five) in terms of the theme of the play and the universality of the message to you in your own life.

- Explain the dramatic change in Macbeth since the beginning of the play. Be sure to include details about the differences in the murders of Duncan and Banquo, the appearance of the ghost, as well as his relationship with Lady Macbeth.

- Explain the dramatic change in Lady Macbeth from the beginning of the play. Be sure to include details about her motivations at the beginning of the play, her feelings towards Macbeth and the murders taking place and finally, her state of mind in Act Five.

- Explain the irony in Macbeth's line: "Infected be the air whereupon they [the witches] ride, / And damned all those who trust them!" from Act Four.

Name _____ Period _____

Macbeth
Final Test: Multiple Choice

Directions: Choose the letter of the BEST response, writing your choice on the answer document or bubble sheet you have been provided.

1. What does "False face must hide what the false heart doth know" mean?
   (A) Your feelings are false.
   (B) You must act out your revenge.
   (C) You do not know how to behave.
   (D) You must hide your true feelings.

2. Lady Macbeth's plan is to blame Duncan's murder on:
   (A) Duncan's guards
   (B) the witches
   (C) Banquo
   (D) Malcolm

3. Why did the witches harm the fat lady's husband
   (A) She wouldn't give them money.
   (B) She wouldn't share her chestnuts.
   (C) She lied to them.
   (D) She told the witches that she didn't believe their prophecies.

4. At the beginning of the play, the war was between:
   (A) Scotland and Sweden
   (B) Scotland and Norway
   (C) England and Scotland
   (D) England and Norway

5. Which character provides comic relief in the play?
   (A) Ross
   (B) Lady Macbeth
   (C) Lennox
   (D) the Porter

6. Which of the following was NOT a prediction given by the apparitions?
   (A) "Beware Macduff"
   (B) "None of woman born shall harm Macbeth"
   (C) Macbeth will never be harmed until Birnam Wood comes to Dunsinane
   (D) "Thou shall get kings, though thou be none"

7. Who joins Malcolm and Macduff to overthrow Macbeth at the end of the play?
   (A) Fleance
   (B) Banquo
   (C) Duncan
   (D) Siward

8. Where is Duncan killed?
   (A) Scone
   (B) Dunsinane
   (C) Inverness
   (D) Birnam Wood

9. Who discovers Duncan's body?
   (A) Macbeth
   (B) Macduff
   (C) Siward
   (D) the Porter

10. What does Lady Macduff call her husband?
    (A) villain
    (B) hero
    (C) traitor
    (D) thief

11. Who becomes King of Scotland at the end of the play?
    (A) Macduff
    (B) Malcolm
    (C) Fleance
    (D) Old Siward

12. Who was "from his mother's womb, untimely ripped"?
    (A) Macduff
    (B) Malcolm
    (C) Fleance
    (D) Young Siward

13. Macbeth sees all of the following apparitions EXCEPT a:
    (A) line of men with mirrors
    (B) crowned child with a tree
    (C) child holding a burning cross
    (D) head with a helmet

14. What is the prophecy given to Banquo?
(A) He will be the father of kings
(B) He will be killed by someone close to him
(C) He will become king
(D) He will be labeled a traitor

15. Lady Macbeth can best be described as:
(A) loving and supportive
(B) vengeful and sympathetic
(C) motherly and driven
(D) ambitious and motivated

16. Which characters flee Scotland in fear of their own lives?
(A) Macduff and Malcolm
(B) Macduff, Malcolm, and Banquo
(C) Fleance and Donalbain
(D) Donalbain, Malcolm, and Macduff

17. Who breaks the news to Macduff that his family was killed?
(A) Macbeth
(B) Lennox
(C) Fleance
(D) Ross

18. Duncan pushes Macbeth over the edge in Act One by announcing that he is:
(A) going to attack England
(B) stripping Macdonwald of his title
(C) demoting Macbeth
(D) making Malcolm the next king of Scotland

19. Banquo can best be described as:
(A) fatherly and loving
(B) loyal and intuitive
(C) vengeful and hateful
(D) naïve and immature

20. As she reads the letter from her husband, Lady Macbeth becomes:
(A) anxious that the king is coming
(B) convinced she wants Duncan dead
(C) nervous that Macbeth will be home early
(D) afraid the witches will visit her

21. How does Macbeth justify killing the King's servants?
(A) He says he watched them kill the king.
(B) He blames them for killing the king.
(C) He said he didn't trust or like them.
(D) He said he was afraid they would kill again.

22. How many witches are in the play?
(A) 2
(B) 3
(C) 4
(D) 5

23. *Macbeth* takes place in:
(A) Scotland
(B) England
(C) Ireland
(D) Wales

24. Who jokes that he is Hell's gatekeeper?
(A) Macbeth
(B) Macduff
(C) the Porter
(D) Ross

25. Macbeth's tragic flaw is his:
(A) ambition
(B) wife
(C) seizures
(D) failing memory

26. When Macbeth is unable, Lady Macbeth:
(A) kills Duncan
(B) plants the bloody daggers
(C) kills the kings servants
(D) explains to Macduff how they found the king dead

27. Who does Malcolm lie to in order to test his allegiance?
(A) Macbeth
(B) Duncan
(C) Macduff
(D) Lennox

28. Duncan's sons are immediately suspected of Duncan's murder because they:
    (A) have blood on their hands
    (B) run away
    (C) find the bloody daggers
    (D) accuse Macbeth of committing the murder

29. At the news of his wife's death, Macbeth:
    (A) breaks down and cries
    (B) vows revenge
    (C) prays
    (D) insists "life goes on"

30. When Lady Macbeth appears sleepwalking in Act Five, she is:
    (A) washing her hands
    (B) drinking a potion
    (C) carrying a knife
    (D) carrying a light

31. Who said [Life] is a tale / Told by an idiot, full of sound and fury / Signifying nothing"?
    (A) Macbeth
    (B) Macduff
    (C) Lady Macbeth
    (D) Banquo

32. Who is the goddess of witchcraft?
    (A) Lady Macbeth
    (B) Lady Macduff
    (C) Hecate
    (D) Hester

33. Who will never be king, but will be the father of kings?
    (A) Macduff
    (B) Banquo
    (C) Macbeth
    (D) Malcolm

34. Who said "Out, damned spot! Out, I say! – One, two. Why, then, 'tis time to do' t. Hell is murky"
    (A) Macbeth
    (B) Lady Macbeth
    (C) Malcolm
    (D) Hecate

35. Who said "Tyrant, show thy face! / If thou be'st slain and with no stroke of mine, / My wife and children's ghosts will haunt me still"?
    (A) Macbeth
    (B) Macduff
    (C) Lady Macduff
    (D) Banquo

36. Who said "A little water clears us of this deed. / How easy is it then"?
    (A) Lady Macbeth
    (B) Macbeth
    (C) Macduff
    (D) Ross

37. Who said "I grant him bloody, / Luxurious, avaricious, false, deceitful, / Sudden, malicious, smacking of every sin / That has a name"?
    (A) Ross
    (B) Lennox
    (C) Macduff
    (D) Malcolm

38. Who said "Fathered he is, and yet he's fatherless"?
    (A) Ross
    (B) Lennox
    (C) Malcolm
    (D) Lady Macduff

39. Who said "Fair is foul and foul is fair"?
    (A) Macbeth
    (B) Macduff
    (C) the Witches
    (D) Banquo's ghost

40. Who said "Come, you spirits / That tend on mortal thoughts, unsex me here, / And fill me from the crown to the topful / Of direst cruelty"?
    (A) Macbeth
    (B) Macduff
    (C) Lady Macbeth
    (D) Lady Macduff

Teacher Guide – Macbeth Literature Guide
About this Macbeth Literature Guide

Not all activities and worksheets in this guide must be used. They are here to help you, so that you have some options to use with your students. **Please do not feel pressure to use everything!** We have worked hard to create a variety of helpful materials for you to choose from. Pick and choose materials that fit the needs of *your* students in *your* classroom, in *your* timeframe! Here are a few notes about his Guide:

1. It is highly recommended that all reading of the play be done in class as a whole group. Interpreting Shakespeare can be very intimidating to most students and having a teacher there to guide them can help allay those fears. One way to effectively do this is to listen to an audio recording. I recommend Macbeth (Arkangel Shakespeare) Unabridged Audiobook, ISBN 978-1932219203.

2. The Pelican Shakespeare edition of *Macbeth* (ISBN 978-0140714784, ©2000) and the *Arden Shakespeare Complete Works* (ISBN 978-1904271031, ©1998) were both consulted for this Guide. There were variations in line numbers, spelling and punctuation throughout.

3. For the *Anticipation/Reaction Activity* on pages 12-13, I encourage you to engage in a class discussion about these statements. You may want to have those who say "Yes" go to one wall or corner of the class, those who say "No" go to another wall or corner, and those who were undecided to stay in their seats. Choose one or two students from each side to defend their point of view. If those who haven't decided like the argument from one side, they can choose to move to that side or the other, but they must explain why they chose the side.

4. Definitions for vocabulary (pgs. 119-120) are given in the form of the context of the play and may not necessarily be the most common or modern usage.

5. Both the *Scene Guide* activities and *Comprehension Check* questions are there to help your students get the most out of the play. Depending upon your students and their needs, you may opt to have them only take notes, only do the Comprehension Check questions, or alternate between the two. Because of the difficulty of Shakespeare's works, it is recommended that students do both, because of the repetition.

6. *Post-Reading Activities and Alternative Assessment* ideas are located on pages 121-122. Again, these are suggestions only. These project ideas can also be used in addition to a written test, or in place of it. Project rubrics are located on pages 126-127. Please note that the rubrics are slightly different: *Project Rubric A* is recommended for projects that have a small written element that does NOT have to be researched. *Project Rubric B* is recommended for projects that include a research component in which sources must be cited.

7. *Essay/Writing Ideas* are located on pages 123-125. Often, having students choose ONE topic from 2-3 essay topics that you have chosen ahead of time in addition to their written test works well. Many of these options can also work as a process essay during your teaching of *Macbeth*.

8. *Journal Ideas and Discussion Topics* (pages 32-33) have also been provided, should you want to include a journal-writing component or discussion panel. Suggestions about when to give prompts have been provided.

9. If you feel uncomfortable or uncertain about interpreting Shakespeare, you might consider using Spark Notes *No Fear Shakespeare/Macbeth* along with this Guide.

Macbeth
Sample Agenda

Our Literature Guides are designed to be used in their sequential entirety, or they may be divided into separate parts. Not all activities must be used, but to achieve full comprehension and mastery of the skills involved, it is recommended that you utilize everything each Guide has to offer. Below is a sample unit plan integrating all aspects of this *Macbeth* Literature Guide. This agenda assumes students have the time to read together as a class. It will need to be modified if you intend to have your students read at home or have them complete a combination of reading in class and at home.

Week One
Day One: Have students complete *Standards Focus: Elements of Drama* (pg. 7)
Day Two: As a class, review *Standards Focus: Literary Elements* (pg. 8). As an activity, you may want to have students choose 5-10 elements and create an example of their own to illustrate the meaning of the literary element. Give *Informational Text: Author Biography and Comprehension Check: Author Biography* (pgs. 14-15) for homework.
Day Three: Review what students learned about Shakespeare and his life. Now is a good time to explore students' fears and insecurities regarding Shakespeare. Lead a discussion, asking students questions such as "What scares you about reading Shakespeare?" or "Why do you think students are required to read Shakespeare?" or "What have you heard about the story of Macbeth?" Now is also a good time to express any fears you have/had about Shakespeare's works, reassuring them that you have this Guide, which can help answer any questions or squelch fears students may have. Have students complete the Anticipation Guide Pre-Reading Activity (pgs. 12-13). Discuss in class.
Day Four: Introduce *Working with Shakespeare's Language* (pgs. 16-17).
Day Five: Have students present their scenes from *Working with Shakespeare's Language* (pages 16-17).

Week Two
Day One: Introduce students to *Appreciating Shakespeare's Language* (pgs. 18-19) and *Glossary of Terms from Macbeth* (pgs. 34-35). Be sure to remind students that the Glossary as well as the Map of 11th Century Scotland (page 28) are there to help them if they get stuck on a word or set of words or want to know where everything is located. It is important also that if you read in class, you model the behavior of using this Glossary when needed. For homework, have students complete *Informational Text: Theater in Shakespeare's Time* and *Comprehension Check: Shakespeare's Theater* (pgs. 20-22)
Day Two: Take time to discuss Shakespeare's Theater, including the set-up (i.e. groundlings, wide appeal of Shakespeare's plays, lack of women). At this point, you may want to have students continue the Informational Text articles either in class or as homework, depending upon your timeframe. These are found on pages (23-27).
Day Three: Introduce and complete *Shakespeare's Style: The Sonnet Form and Iambic Pentameter* (pgs. 29-30). Students may have to finish for homework.
Day Four: Give *Shakespeare's Style: Sonnet Quiz* (pg. 31). Introduce *Pre-Reading Activities* (pgs. 10-11). Allow students to gain a better understanding of Shakespeare's time by completing and/or working on a project from this list either before or during your reading of *Macbeth*. Give due dates for projects.
Day Five: Introduce *List of Allusions* (pgs. 36-37). Review what an allusion is, and remind students that this list is available if they don't understand a reference when reading. Again, be sure to model using this list when reading in class. Give either the *Vocabulary List*

without definitions (pg. 38) or the *Vocabulary List with Definitions* (pg. 119). If you choose to give the list without definitions, have students look up the vocabulary words, keeping their own personal dictionary for use with worksheets and vocabulary activities.

Week Three
Day One: Introduce the *Scene Guide* (pg. 39). Students will be completing a guide like this for each act as they read. You will want to model the note-taking for the first few scenes. When reading in class, be sure to give students time to complete their Scene Guide after each scene. Discuss any problems, and talk about the important events to make sure students understand this process. Begin reading Act One and after reading the Prologue, review the sample scene guide. Have students begin using the Scene Guide for Act One to take notes as they read. At this time, you may want to introduce *Journal Ideas/Discussion Topics* pgs. 32-33 each day before reading or as you have the time.
Day Two: Continue reading and completing the *Act One Scene Guide*.
Day Three: Continue reading and completing the *Act One Scene Guide*. Once the class has completed reading Act One, give *Act One Comprehension Check* questions (pgs. 42-43) either for homework, or to complete in class.
Day Four: Complete either the *Standards Focus: Dialogue, Monologue, and More* (pgs. 44-46) or Standards Focus: Mood (pgs. 47-48) or both, if you have the time. (Give yourself at least an extra day to complete.)
Day Five: Complete *Assessment Preparation: Context Clues* (pgs. 49-52), if you are having students work with vocabulary.

Week Four
Day One: Give *Act One Quiz* (pgs. 90-91) and *Act One Vocabulary Quiz* (pg. 92). Begin reading Act Two and completing *Act Two Scene Guide* (pgs. 53-54).
Day Two: Continue reading Act Two and completing the *Act Two Scene Guide*.
Day Three: Once the class has completed reading Act Two, give *Act Two Comprehension Check* questions (pgs. 55-56) either for homework, or to complete in class.
Day Four: Complete *Standards Focus: Figurative Language* (pgs. 57-58) and/or *Standards Focus: Plot and Conflict* (pgs. 59-61) or both, depending upon your students and your timeframe.
Day Five: Complete *Assessment Preparation: Word Usage* (pg. 62) if you are having students work with vocabulary.

Week Five
Day One: Give *Act Two Quiz* (pgs. 93-94 and *Act Two Vocabulary Quiz* (pg. 95). Begin reading Act Three and completing *Act Three Scene Guide* (pgs. 63-64).
Day Two: Continue reading Act Three and completing the *Act Three Scene Guide*.
Day Three: Continue reading Act Three and completing the *Act Three Scene Guide*. Once the class has completed reading Act Three, give *Act Three Comprehension Check* questions (pgs. 65-66) either for homework, or to complete in class
Day Four: Complete *Standards Focus: Irony* (pgs. 67-68) and/or *Standards Focus: Characterization* (pgs. 69-71) or both, depending upon your students and your timeframe.
Day Five: Complete *Assessment Preparation: Vocabulary Builders* (pg. 72) if you are having students work with vocabulary.

Week Six
Day One: Give *Act Three Quiz* (pgs. 96-97) and *Act Three Vocabulary Quiz* (pg. 98). Begin reading Act Four and completing the *Act Four Scene Guide* (pgs. 73).
Day Two: Continue reading Act Four and completing the *Act Four Scene Guide*.

Day Three: Continue reading Act Four and completing the *Act Four Scene Guide*. Once the class has completed reading Act Four, give *Act Four Comprehension Check* questions (pg. 74) either for homework, or to complete in class.

Day Four: Complete *Standards Focus: Character Analysis* (pgs. 75-76) and/or *Standards Focus: Motif* (pgs. 77-78) or both, depending upon your students and your timeframe.

Day Five: Complete *Assessment Preparation: Vocabulary Extension* (pgs. 79) if you are having students work with vocabulary.

Week Seven

Day One: Give *Act Four Quiz* (pgs. 99-100) and *Act Four Vocabulary Quiz* (pg. 101). Begin reading Act Five and completing the *Act Five Scene Guide* (pgs. 80-81).

Day Two: Continue reading Act Five and completing the *Act Five Scene Guide*.

Day Three: Continue reading Act Five and completing the *Act Five Scene Guide*. Once the class has completed reading Act Five, give *Act Five Comprehension Check* questions (pgs. 82-83) either for homework, or to complete in class.

Day Four: Complete *Standards Focus: Tragedy and the Tragic Hero* (pg. 84) and/or *Standards Focus: Theme* (pgs. 85-87) or both, depending upon your students and your timeframe.

Day Five: Complete *Assessment Preparation: Vocabulary in Context* (pgs. 88-89) if you are having students work with vocabulary.

Week Eight

Day One: Give *Act Five Quiz* (pgs. 102-103) and *Act Five Vocabulary Quiz* (pg. 104). Begin review of entire play. You may want to have students do the *Just for Fun! Crossword Puzzle* for review (pg. 105). Introduce *Post-Reading Activities and Alternative Assessment* (pgs. 121-122). Give parameters for completion, and allow students to choose which project they would like to do. Assign due dates.

Day Two: Give either version of the Final Test (pgs. 106-109 or pgs. 110-112). Some alternates to these tests are a project from the *Post-Reading and Alternative Assessment* ideas (pgs. 121-122), an essay exam from the *Essay/Writing Ideas* (pgs. 123-125) or any combination of the three test types. Two different *Project Rubrics* are on pages 126-127; a *Response to Literature Essay Rubric* is on pages 128-129.

Days Three-Five: Allow students time in class to work on their Post-Reading activities or Essay/Writing assignments.

Macbeth
Summary of the Play

Act One

The play begins ominously, as three witches meet, make mysterious statements, "Fair is foul and foul is fair," then agree to meet again. Scotland and Norway are at war. Macbeth is hailed as a hero, killing Norway's Macdonwald. Duncan orders the execution of the Thane of Cawdor for his treason, and gives Macbeth the title of Thane of Cawdor for his bravery and honor to the king. Later, the three witches greet Macbeth and Banquo in the woods and prophesy that Macbeth will be Thane of Cawdor, Thane of Glamis, and king. They also say that Banquo will not be king, but that he shall be the father of kings. Ross and Angus show up, explaining that the Thane of Glamis has been convicted of treason, and Duncan has now named Macbeth the Thane of Glamis. Two out of the three predictions have now come true, and this intrigues and excites Macbeth. Malcolm tells Duncan that Cawdor has been executed and Duncan tells Macbeth how embarrassed he is of his blind trust of the old Thane.

Duncan promises Macbeth his just rewards for his loyalty, but then, to Macbeth's surprise and disappointment, Duncan proclaims Malcolm to be successor to the throne. Duncan decides to visit Macbeth at Inverness to celebrate his promotion, unaware of the evil thoughts Macbeth is entertaining. Later, Lady Macbeth reads a letter from Macbeth, telling her of the witches' prophecy. She immediately sees the opportunity to become Queen, and promises to encourage her husband to act boldly, or she will commit the act of murder herself. Duncan arrives at Macbeth's castle, unaware of the impending danger, and Lady Macbeth greets him pleasantly, putting on the appearance of a good hostess. Macbeth and Lady Macbeth make their plans to kill the king, but in a moment of weakness, Macbeth doubts his courage to kill the king. Lady Macbeth calls him a coward, and rather coldly and rudely, talks him into action.

Act Two

Banquo admits to his son that he is having dreams about the witches' predictions. Meanwhile, back at Inverness, Macbeth hallucinates seeing a bloody dagger leading him to kill Duncan. He follows the dagger and goes to kill the king. Lady Macbeth has been drinking and she reveals she has drugged the guards. Macbeth tells her the king is dead. Macbeth did not plant the daggers, and because of the shock of what he has done, he refuses to go back to the scene and plant the daggers. So Lady Macbeth returns to the scene to bloody the sleeping guards' pillows and to plant the daggers on them. Macbeth and Lady Macbeth hear knocking at the door, and it greatly unnerves Macbeth. Lady Macbeth tells Macbeth to clean up and get into his sleeping clothes to pretend that he has been sleeping. The knocking continues and the drunk Porter goes to answer it, after a short speech about the effects of alcohol and being in hell. Macduff and Lennox come to wake the king, as ordered. Macduff discovers Duncan has been murdered. Macbeth admits killing the guards, who were believed to have killed the king. Duncan's sons, Malcolm and Donalbain fear that they are next to be killed, so Malcolm flees to England and Donalbain flees to Ireland. Ross and an old man talk about the evil looming —the horses are even eating each other. Because of their hasty disappearance, Macbeth suggests that Malcolm and Donalbain must have killed their father. Since there is no one to take the throne, Macbeth, because of his "heroic" deeds, will be crowned king.

Act Three

Banquo suspects Macbeth of foul play; Macbeth knows Banquo suspects him, and therefore, Banquo becomes Macbeth's next target. Macbeth finds out where Banquo will be, and in a soliloquy, expresses his jealousy and fear of Banquo. He arranges the murder of Banquo and Fleance with two hired murderers. Macbeth's doubts and fears are becoming stronger, and Lady Macbeth tries to encourage him by telling him to hide his fears with a happy disposition, especially since they are having guests that evening. Banquo and Fleance are ambushed; Banquo is killed, but Fleance escapes. A murderer arrives at Inverness to tell Macbeth that Banquo is dead, but that Fleance has escaped. At the banquet, Banquo's ghost appears, and Macbeth is the only one who can see it. Lady Macbeth excuses her husband's behavior, saying he has had these fits since his youth, and they will pass. The ghost appears and disappears several times, taunting Macbeth, who begins to speak aloud to the ghost. Fearing that he will say too much, Lady Macbeth tells everyone to leave. Hecate, the queen of the witches, chastises the three witches for their involvement in Macbeth's life. Lennox reveals his suspicions of Macbeth; a lord tells him that Macduff has gone to England to gather support to overthrow Macbeth.

Act Four

The three witches prepare their spell. Macbeth arrives, thirsty for more information about his future. Three apparitions appear: an armed head warns "beware Macduff"; a bloody child says "none of woman born" shall hurt Macbeth; a child crowned says that nothing will happen until Birnam Wood moves to Dunsinane. Lennox tells Macbeth that Macduff has gone to England. Macbeth orders Macduff and his family killed. Ross delivers the news to Lady Macduff that her husband has gone to England. Lady Macduff is angry Macduff left them, and tells her son that his father was a traitor and is dead. An unknown messenger warns her to leave, but the murderers kill Macduff's son, and then Lady Macduff. In England, Malcolm is unsure of Macduff's sincerity, so he tests him, stating that if he were to take over, he would act exactly like Macbeth. As Macduff goes to leave, Malcolm reveals Macduff has passed the test, and agrees to gather the King of England's support to overthrow Macbeth. Ross arrives with news of Macduff's family; Macduff swears revenge.

Act Five

A doctor has been called to deal with Lady Macbeth's sleepwalking. Lady Macbeth appears, trying to wash her hands of the blood of those she and husband have killed. She reveals information about the murder of Duncan, Banquo and Macduff's family. The doctor says he cannot help—she needs divine intervention. Meanwhile, the Scottish and English armies are preparing for war. Macbeth, nervous about the battle, reminds himself of the witches prophecies. He is reassured that none of woman born shall harm him. Macbeth finds out that many of his countrymen are against him; he calls for his armor and vows to fight to the end. Malcolm orders his soldiers to each hold a branch "of Birnam" to camouflage themselves. They advance. Macbeth finds out that Lady Macbeth is dead, presumably by her own hand; Macbeth is practically indifferent to the news. Macbeth gives a speech about the quickness of life and how we are all but insignificant moments of life walking the earth. A messenger brings news that Birnam Wood is moving toward Dunsinane. Recognizing the prophecy, Macbeth fears the end, but still clings to the idea that none of woman born shall harm him. Macbeth fights and kills Young Siward, and is revived and reassured. Macduff arrives and reveals that he was "untimely ripped" from his mother, presumably a primitive Caesarean section. After a short battle, Macduff kills Macbeth, cuts off his head, and reveals it to all, declaring that Malcolm is now the rightful King of Scotland.

Macbeth
Vocabulary with Definitions

Act One

1. **chalice**: n. a cup or goblet
2. **chastise**: v. to punish by beating; to criticize severely
3. **compunctious**: adj. deserving of shame; deeply wrong
4. **dwindle**: v. to make or become gradually less until little remains
5. **harbinger**: n. one that indicates or foreshadows what is to come; forerunner
6. **implored**: v. 1) involved by logical necessity; entailed; 2) appealed to; beseeched
7. **ingratitude**: n. lack of gratitude; ungratefulness
8. **interim**: n. a period between two events
9. **mettle**: n. strength of character; determination
10. **minion**: n. a submissive follower or dependent
11. **plight**: n. a difficult or adverse situation
12. **prophetic**: adj. of, or a characteristic of, a prophet or prophecy
13. **surmise**: v. to infer with little evidence; guess; conjecture n. an idea or opinion base on little evidence
14. **trifles**: n. things of little importance or value; small amounts
15. **withered**: adj. dried up or shriveled, as if from a loss of moisture

Act Two

1. **allegiance**: n. loyalty to a ruler or country
2. **augment**: v. to add something in order to make it larger or more substantial
3. **carousing**: v. drinking and becoming noisy
4. **clamored**: v. shouted and demanded noisily
5. **dire**: adj. a scvere, serious, or desperate situation or circumstance
6. **gild**: v. to cover with a substance; usually gold or gold-like
7. **lamenting(s)**: n. expression(s) of grief or sorrow

8. **malice**: n. intention or desire to cause great harm to someone
9. **palpable**: adj. able to be felt, touched
10. **parley**: v. to talk or negotiate; speak with
11. **predominance**: n. appearing as most important, powerful; strongest or most common in number or amount
12. **provoke**: v. to stir emotion in someone; arouse
13. **quenched**: v. satisfied thirst
14. **scruples**: n. moral or ethical considerations
15. **summons**: n. calling for service or action

Act Three

1. **affliction**: n. a condition of great physical or mental distress
2. **chide**: v. to put down; to tell someone off
3. **cloistered**: adj. secluded from the world
4. **dauntless**: adj. fearless, unable to be intimidated
5. **fruitless**: adj. unproductive or unsuccessful
6. **grapple**: v. wrestle or struggle with
7. **incensed**: adj. made extremely angry
8. **jovial**: adj. cheerful; happy
9. **malevolence**: n. great evil or harm
10. **pious**: adj. religious; devout
11. **purged**: v. removed something undesirable or imperfect
12. **scepter**: n. a ceremonial staff or rod
13. **sundry**: adj. various; miscellaneous
14. **tyrant**: n. a harsh or cruel leader
15. **vile**: adj. disgusting; wicked; unpleasant

Act Four

1. **antic**: n. a childish act or gesture
2. **avaricious**: adj. having extreme desire for wealth; greedy
3. **bodements**: n. omens; foreshadowing
4. **cistern**: n. a tank for storing water
5. **desolate**: adj. without inhabitants; deserted
6. **dolor**: n. intense sadness
7. **entrails**: n. internal organs, especially the intestines
8. **laudable**: adj. praiseworthy; commendable
9. **malady**: n. a physical or psychological disorder or disease
10. **pernicious**: adj. deadly or destructive
11. **quarry**: n. an animal or bird that is hunted
12. **relish**: v. to enjoy or take pleasure in something
13. **resolute**: adj. having or motivated by determination
14. **sovereignty**: n. supreme authority or rule
15. **teems**: v. has an extremely large number or amount; overflows

Act Five

1. **agitation**: n. violent shaking or stirring; disturbance
2. **arbitrate**: v. to judge or settle a dispute
3. **condemn**: v. to consider a person guilty
4. **divine**: adj. connecting or relating to God or gods
5. **fortifies**: v. makes stronger
6. **fury**: n. uncontrollable anger or rage
7. **gentry**: n. people of good family or high social position
8. **mar**: v. to damage or spoil
9. **murky**: adj. thick, gloomy, and hard to see through
10. **perturbation**: n. something that disturbs or makes one anxious
11. **pestered**: v. annoyed constantly; bothered
12. **pristine**: adj. remaining in a pure state; uncorrupted
13. **recoil**: v. move back suddenly
14. **revolts**: n. rebellions against authority
15. **upbraid**: v. to criticize sharply; to reprimand

Name _____ Period _____

Macbeth
Post-Reading Activities and Alternative Assessment
The following are suggested project ideas and activities to supplement the study of *Macbeth* **after** reading the play. These projects can be used as a post-reading activity or for alternative assessment rather than a written test for differentiation.

1. Choose a scene or an act from the play to "translate" into text-message "language." *Note: Although this activity can be fun and is not necessarily the best use of language, it must accurately tell the story.*

2. Write a rap "translation" of the witches' scene (Act Three, Scene 1), Macbeth seeing the dagger (Act Two, Scene 1), Macbeth's "Out, Out" soliloquy (Act Five, Scene 5) or any other significant scene from the play. *Note: Although this activity can be fun and is not necessarily the best use of language, it must accurately tell the story.*

3. Research supernatural creatures, including those characters found in folklore, legends, and other stories, such as demons, zombies, witches, chupacabra, bigfoot, the Boogeyman, ghouls, ghosts, vampires, sprites, elves, trolls, dragons, etc. Put together your findings in some format, such as a website, brochure, poster, PowerPoint, etc.

4. Use the Internet to compile an annotated list of helpful websites related to the study of *Macbeth*. Find sites about Shakespeare, the play itself, Elizabethan England, the Globe Theater. etc. Write a short description of what each site has to offer. Be discriminating; do not include just any site you come across.

5. Choose a scene to reenact in modern day, or in a setting of your choice. You must "translate" the lines for each character into modern English, and set the scene, complete with minimal costumes and props. Imagine what Macbeth might look like as a 1920s gangster, going after a Tommy-Gun instead of a knife in the dagger scene! Be creative! Each student in your group must have a role in addition to the acting, such as director, prop master, costumer, scene designer, etc. For more interest, create a video and post it on YouTube! Be sure to invite your administrators to watch it!

6. Create a visual tableau of the important scenes of Macbeth. Use images from the Internet (be sure to cite your sources), or free clip art, or original drawings.

7. Create a newspaper called *The Scotland Caller (or a creative title of your own invention)*. Include local news (such as the murders of Duncan, the crowning of Macbeth, the death of Banquo and Macduff's family, an advice column, classified ads, a "fashion" column, gossip, Reader's Opinion column, sports news, recipes and restaurant reviews, announcements, advertisements, weather, a crossword, the funny page, etc. All of your newspaper articles should relate to the time period and the themes of *Macbeth*.

8. Create a board game that includes the following:
   a. Game Cards (at least 20) which contain quotations from the play
   b. Game Pieces (at least 4 different ones) representing different characters of your choice
   c. Game Board, complete with your art work, that relates to some aspect of the theme(s) of the play
   d. Typed directions on how to play the game, the object of the game, and how to win

9. You are a psychologist and your patient is a character of your choice from *Macbeth*. He or she has come seeking advice. What questions would you ask your patient? What

advice would you give? Compose notes and/or a tape recording of your thoughts from ten "sessions." Also consider dream analysis and role-playing exercises. You must have at least ten consecutive sessions and include a one-page final diagnosis/recommendation for your patient.

10. Do a "Paper Bag" report on Macbeth, Lady Macbeth, Banquo, Macduff, Lady Macduff, Lennox, Malcolm, Fleance, or any other character. Include in your paper bag ten items of significance to the character. Decorate the paper bag to represent the most important theme or lesson for that character. Write a paragraph for each item, telling why you chose the items and how they are significant symbols of the character. Give your paper bag report orally.

11. Create a "Wanted" poster for Macbeth. Be sure to include a description of Macbeth, a picture, crime committed and situation, weapons used, where he was last seen, what he was wearing, etc.

12. Create a 15-20 page children's book of *Macbeth*. Using large, easy to read font and short, elementary-level words. Tell about the story's important events and characters, making sure the themes come across to the reader. Include pictures on each page that depict the story.

13. Pretend you are a costume designer for a theatrical version of the play. Make a journal of the costumes for each of the following characters from the play: Macbeth, Lady Macbeth, Macduff, Malcolm, Banquo, Duncan, and Lennox. Each drawing must be on an 8 ½" by 11" paper, with fabric swatches attached. Write a one-page explanation of how these particular costumes are representative of each character, including when in the play they would wear the costume.

14. Choose a monologue to perform in class. You must dress in an appropriate costume and use appropriate props. LINES MUST BE MEMORIZED.

15. Use a computer program or draw/paint an original CD cover depicting one of the themes in *Macbeth*. On your CD, include a compilation of 15 songs (both new and old) you feel best represent the most important scenes of the play. Put together a report of your songs, including the name of the song, artist, and album the song came from, a copy of the lyrics and a minimum one paragraph explanation of why you chose each song to represent a particular theme, and which event or incident the song represents. For example, you may choose a specific song for when the apparitions appear to Macbeth. What song would be appropriate to represent the mood during this scene? Why?

16. Research the different theaters in Shakespeare's time, including the Globe and the Rose theaters. Create a 3-D presentation of one of the theaters along with a report covering the history of the theater, theater patrons, performances, life of the theater, etc.

17. Gather a collection of published poetry based upon the play. Put the poetry together in a folder, complete with pictures and biographical references. For an added challenge, write a poem of your own and include it, too.

18. Compile a collection of modern references to Macbeth. These can be references in movies, books, songs, etc. Put these together in a portfolio format such as a website, blog, poster, etc.

Macbeth
Essay/Writing Ideas

For this Guide, essay and writing activities are two different types of writing assignments. For the essay ideas, students should answer the questions in a succinct, comprehensive, MINIMUM five-paragraph essay. Each answer should be at least 2-3 typed, double-spaced pages, or within the guidelines you provide.

Following the *Essay Ideas* are *Writing Ideas* that do not necessarily follow the "essay" format. For the writing ideas, follow the directions given.

Essay Ideas

1. Is Macbeth a villain or a victim of his fate, wife, the supernatural, etc.? Take a position on whether you believe Macbeth was destined to be evil, or whether other things influenced him to become evil. Is he completely evil in all his dealings and relationships, or is there more to him? How does he change throughout the play? What is his tragic flaw? Identify his transition from hero to tyrant. Be sure to find examples from the text to support your response.

2. Who is to blame for the deaths of Duncan, Banquo, Macduff's family, Lady Macbeth, etc.? Is it the witches? Macbeth himself? Lady Macbeth? Fate? Or something else? In a well-written five-paragraph persuasive essay, convince your reader who is to blame for Macbeth's bloody actions. Be sure to use evidence from the text to support your response.

3. Explore the relationship between Macbeth and Lady Macbeth. Do they have a good marriage? Are they in love? Are they equal? How does their relationship seem to work? How does it shift over time? How does Macbeth react to Lady Macbeth's death? What does this reveal about their relationship at this point? Be sure to use evidence from the text to support your response.

4. Discuss the use of hallucinations and visions in the play. Why do you think Shakespeare included these visual effects? How do these visions and hallucinations help to shape the character and his/her state of mind? Give details from the text to support your response.

5. The idea of masculinity and manhood is a theme in Macbeth. Identify statements of masculinity and "being a man" and how they are defined in the play. How are gender roles defined? How are these roles reversed or shifted throughout the play?

6. Compare and contrast the characters of Macbeth and Macduff. Consider their personalities, relationships, and what motivates each character. Is one man good and the other evil, or are they both good or both evil, as outside influences affect their decisions? What kinds of relationships do they have with their families? How are their views on life similar or different? Explain.

7. Compare and contrast the characters of Macbeth and Banquo. Consider the prophecies they were given and how each dealt with them. Is one man good and the other evil, or are they both good or both evil, as outside influences affect their decisions? How are their views on the prophecies and life in general similar or different? Explain.

8. Analyze the character of Lady Macbeth. What is her role in Macbeth's life? How does her role change? Is she an evil human being, or are there other forces that drive her? How does she change? Why? Is she to blame for Macbeth's demise? Could such a woman exist

in today's society? Would she still be capable of the same power over her husband? Or might she have even more? Explain your response.

9. Discuss any of the motifs of blood, water, sleep, weather/nature, masculinity, light and dark. Find quotes to support the use of the motif throughout the play. Be sure to include an analysis of how the motif contributes to the theme(s) of the play.

10. How does Shakespeare use the technique of dramatic irony in *Macbeth*? Give examples from the text to support your response.

11. Explore the relationships between spouses in *Macbeth*. Look at the relationship between Macbeth and Lady Macbeth, and Macduff and Lady Macduff. What do they all have in common? What differentiates them? How equal are the relationships? Explain in detail, giving examples from the text to support your response.

Writing Ideas

1. Research the Gunpowder Plot of 1605, a plan to assassinate King James I. In a well-written five-paragraph (minimum) essay, compare and contrast the similarities and differences between the Gunpowder Plot and the assassination of King Duncan in Macbeth. You MUST cite your sources of information in a bibliography.

2. Conduct an interview with one of the characters from *Macbeth*. For those who died, the interview can be when the character was alive, or after his or her death. Write at least 10 questions that will give the character a chance to tell his or her story from his or her point of view. You may ask questions, challenge a situation, express a complaint or make a suggestion. Then answer the questions in the persona of the character you chose, using insight into the character and details from the story to support your response.

3. Write a diary from either Macbeth or Lady Macbeth's point of view. You are writing in the character of Macbeth or Lady Macbeth. Choose 5-6 important events from the play and respond to each event as the character would respond. The diary should accurately reflect both the events of the story as well as the character's state of mind.

4. Using correct letter format, write a letter from Lady Macbeth attempting to explain her feelings about being queen, talking Macbeth out of further killings, or a "goodbye" letter before she kills herself. Be sure that you are in the persona of Lady Macbeth. Letter should be at least one page, and supported with details from the story.

5. Write the obituaries for either Duncan, Banquo, Lady Macbeth, or Macbeth. Be sure to include their important life accomplishments, as well as information about how they died, and what services will be held. Each must be at least a paragraph long. For an extra challenge, write one or both obituaries in sonnet form. Remember that a Shakespearean sonnet has 14 lines with 5 iambs/10 syllables each line.

6. Add a new character to the play. Why would he or she be added? What would he or she contribute to the plot? Rewrite a scene from the play that includes your character. Your character must have lines in the scene, and the scene must make sense in the context of the play.

7. Write about what you would have done in the same situation, had you been one of the characters in *Macbeth*. Be sure to include the name of the character, as well as the specific way you would have handled the situation.

8. Write an alternate ending to the play. What if Macbeth (or Lady Macbeth) had lived? What if they had both lived? What would happen next? What would their married life be like? You choose from where the story changes and what happens to each character.

9. Write a letter to a student who has never read *Macbeth*, giving your impressions, thoughts and insights into the play. Be sure to use correct letter format and include information about characters, a short summary, explanation of themes and your opinion of the book. Also give any hints or ideas that worked to help you understand the story better.

10. Select what you consider the most important episode in *Macbeth*. Why do you feel this is the most important episode? Explain what happened and how you feel this incident or situation affected the play as a whole.

11. Write a 14-line sonnet expressing one of the themes of the play and/or your personal perspective or feelings about Shakespeare or *Macbeth*.

12. What changes would you suggest for *Macbeth* to make it more understandable or enjoyable? What appealed and didn't appeal to you in the play? Make suggestions for changes, explain why you would make the changes, and explain how these changes would improve the story.

13. Create a crossword puzzle or word search for *Macbeth*. The word game must have at least twenty clues and an answer key. You can use character names, vocabulary words, unusual words, or plot items in your project.

14. Compare and contrast the play and the movie adaptations(s) of *Macbeth*, including the Polanski (1971) version (warning—contains nudity), the 1978 version with Ian McKellen and Judi Dench, the 1998 version with Sean Pertwee, or the Australian 2006 version with Sam Worthington. Critique the casting of characters. What do you think about the direction, such as the decision to leave parts of the book out or to add scenes to the film? How well did the director capture the important themes and ideas of the play?

15. Research Elizabethan Era food, clothing, social classes, and household items. In poster format, include information about each. Be sure to cover each aspect and illustrate with pictures for full points. You MUST cite your sources of information in a bibliography.

16. Compare a character in *Macbeth* with a character from another piece of literature. Explain the similarities and differences between these two characters.

17. Gather and analyze two sonnets or poems by Shakespeare or one of his contemporaries, such as John Donne, Thomas Heywood, Ben Jonson, Thomas Kyd, Christopher Marlowe, or Edmund Spenser.

Project Rubric A

Category	Score of 5	Score of 4	Score of 3	Score of 2	Score of 1	Score
Required Elements	Includes all of the required elements as stated in the directions.	Includes all but one or two of the required elements as stated in the directions.	Missing 3 or 4 of the required elements as stated in the directions.	Missing 5 or 6 of the required elements as stated in the directions.	Project does not follow the directions.	
Graphics, Pictures	All pictures, drawings, or graphics are appropriate and add to the enjoyment of the project.	Some pictures, drawings, or graphics are included, are appropriate, and add to the enjoyment of the project.	A few pictures, drawings, or graphics are included and are appropriate to the project.	A few pictures, drawings, or graphics are included, but may not be appropriate to the project, or may be distracting.	Pictures or drawings are not used and/or are inappropriate or distracting to the project.	
Creativity	Exceptionally clever and unique; design and presentation enhance the project.	Clever at times; thoughtfully and uniquely presented.	A few original or clever touches enhance the project.	Little evidence of uniqueness, individuality, and/or effort.	No evidence of creativity or effort. Project is not unique.	
Neatness, Appeal	Exceptionally neat and attractive; typed or very neatly hand-written, appropriate use of color, particularly neat in design and layout.	Neat and attractive; typed or neatly handwritten, good use of color, good design and layout.	Generally neat and attractive; handwritten, some use of color, some problems in design and layout.	Distractingly messy or disorganized; handwritten; little use of color; several problems in design and layout.	Work shows no pride or effort. Project is incomplete, illegible, or particularly messy and unattractive.	
Grammar, Spelling, Mechanics	Little to no problems with grammar, spelling, and mechanics. Project was clearly proofread.	A few problems with grammar, spelling, or mechanics. Errors are minor and do not distract from the project.	Several errors in grammar, spelling, or mechanics. Errors can be slightly distracting at times.	Several problems with grammar, spelling, or mechanics. Errors are distracting.	Many problems with grammar, spelling, or mechanics. Mistakes clearly show project was not proofread.	

Comments:

Final Score: _____ **out of 25**

Project Rubric B

Category	Score of 5	Score of 4	Score of 3	Score of 2	Score of 1	Score
Required Elements	Includes all of the required elements as stated in the directions.	Includes all but one or two of the required elements as stated in the directions.	Missing 3 or 4 of the required elements as stated in the directions.	Missing 5 or 6 of the required elements as stated in the directions.	Project does not follow the directions.	
Creativity	Exceptionally clever and unique; design and presentation enhance the project.	Clever at times; thoughtfully and uniquely presented.	A few original or clever touches enhance the project.	Little evidence of uniqueness, individuality, and/or effort.	No evidence of creativity or effort. Project is not unique.	
Neatness, Appeal	Exceptionally neat and attractive; typed or very neatly hand-written, appropriate use of color, particularly neat in design and layout.	Neat and attractive; typed or neatly handwritten, good use of color, good design and layout.	Generally neat and attractive; handwritten, some use of color, some problems in design and layout.	Distractingly messy or disorganized; handwritten; little use of color; several problems in design and layout.	Work shows no pride or effort. Project is incomplete, illegible, or particularly messy and unattractive.	
Grammar, Spelling, Mechanics	Little to no problems with grammar, spelling, and mechanics. Project was clearly proofread.	A few problems with grammar, spelling, or mechanics. Errors are minor and do not distract from the project.	Several errors in grammar, spelling, or mechanics. Errors can be slightly distracting at times.	Several problems with grammar, spelling, or mechanics. Errors are distracting.	Many problems with grammar, spelling, or mechanics. Mistakes clearly show project was not proofread.	
Citation of Sources	All graphics, pictures, and written work are original, or if they have been obtained from an outside source, have been properly cited.	All graphics, pictures, and written work that are not original or have been obtained from an outside source have been cited, with a few problems.	All graphics, pictures, and written work that are not original or have been obtained from an outside source have been cited, with several problems.	Some attempt has been made to give credit for unoriginal graphics, pictures, and written work.	No attempt has been made to give credit for unoriginal graphics, pictures, and written work.	

Comments:

Final Score: _____ out of 25

Response to Literature Rubric

Adapted from the **California Writing Assessment Rubric**
California Department of Education, Standards and Assessment Division

Score of 4
- ☐ Clearly addresses all parts of the writing task.
- ☐ Provides a meaningful thesis and thoughtfully supports the thesis and main ideas with facts, details, and/or explanations.
- ☐ Maintains a consistent tone and focus and a clear sense of purpose and audience.
- ☐ Illustrates control in organization, including effective use of transitions.
- ☐ Provides a variety of sentence types and uses precise, descriptive language.
- ☐ Contains few, if any, errors in the conventions of the English language (grammar, punctuation, capitalization, spelling). These errors do not interfere with the reader's understanding of the writing.
- ☐ Demonstrates a *clear* understanding of the ambiguities, nuances, and complexities of the text.
- ☐ Develops interpretations that demonstrate a thoughtful, comprehensive, insightful grasp of the text, and supports these judgments with specific references to various texts.
- ☐ Draws well-supported inferences about the effects of a literary work on its audience.
- ☐ Provides *specific* textual examples and/or personal knowledge and details to support the interpretations and inferences.

Score of 3
- ☐ Addresses all parts of the writing task.
- ☐ Provides a thesis and supports the thesis and main ideas with mostly relevant facts, details, and/or explanations.
- ☐ Maintains a generally consistent tone and focus and a general sense of purpose and audience.
- ☐ Illustrates control in organization, including *some* use of transitions.
- ☐ Includes a variety of sentence types and *some* descriptive language.
- ☐ Contains some errors in the conventions of the English language. These errors do not interfere with the reader's understanding of the writing.
- ☐ Develops interpretations that demonstrate a comprehensive grasp of the text and supports these interpretations with references to various texts.
- ☐ Draws supported inferences about the effects of a literary work on its audience.
- ☐ Supports judgments with some specific references to various texts and/or personal knowledge.
- ☐ Provides textual examples and details to support the interpretations.

Score of 2

- ☐ Addresses *only parts* of the writing task.
- ☐ *Suggests* a central idea with *limited* facts, details, and/or explanation.
- ☐ Demonstrates *little* understanding of purpose and audience.
- ☐ Maintains an *inconsistent* point of view, focus, and/or organizational structure which may include *ineffective or awkward* transitions that do not unify important ideas.
- ☐ Contains *several errors* in the conventions of the English language. These errors may interfere with the reader's understanding of the writing.
- ☐ Develops interpretations that demonstrate a limited grasp of the text.
- ☐ Includes interpretations that *lack* accuracy or coherence as related to ideas, premises, or images from the literary work.
- ☐ Draws *few* inferences about the effects of a literary work on its audience.
- ☐ Supports judgments with *few, if any*, references to various text and/or personal knowledge.

Score of 1

- ☐ Addresses *only one* part of the writing task.
- ☐ *Lacks* a thesis or central idea but may contain *marginally related* facts, details, and/or explanations.
- ☐ Demonstrates *no* understanding of purpose and audience.
- ☐ *Lacks* a clear point of view, focus, organizational structure, and transitions that unify important ideas.
- ☐ Includes *no* sentence variety; sentences are simple.
- ☐ Contains *serious errors* in the conventions of the English language. These errors interfere with the reader's understanding of the writing.
- ☐ Develops interpretations that demonstrate *little* grasp of the text.
- ☐ *Lacks* an interpretation or *may* be a simple retelling of the text.
- ☐ *Lacks* inferences about the effects of a literary work on its audience.
- ☐ *Fails* to support judgments with references to various text and/or personal knowledge.
- ☐ *Lacks* textual examples and details.

Answer Key

Note: Answers may not be given in complete sentences, as most student answers should be.

Page 7: Standards Focus: Elements of Drama
Students' original quizzes will vary widely.

Pages 10-11: Pre-Reading Ideas and Activities
Creations and products will always vary widely. Allow room for independent thinking and ingenuity.

Pages 12-13: Anticipation Guide Pre-Reading Activity
Answers are highly personal and will vary.

Page 15: Comprehension Check: Author Biography
1. 1564; Stratford-upon-Avon, England
2. *Answer will vary. Sample student answer: Shakespeare was a powerful writer whose timeless, classic works are still read and enjoyed today.*
3. 18; She was older and pregnant at the time they got married.
4. *Answer will vary. Sample student answer: Shakespeare's first child, Susanna, was born in 1583; two years later, twins Hamnet and Judith were born. In 1596, Hamnet died of unknown causes. The loss was said to have affected William deeply, his grief and loss expressed in his writing.*
5. He was an actor.
6. He died on his birthday.
7. facts; dates and historical information is given
8. chronological; events are in order
9. *Answers will vary.*
10. *Answers will vary.*

Page 16: Working with Shakespeare's Language
Scenes will vary widely.

Pages 20-22: Exploring Expository Writing: Theater in Shakespeare's Time *Answers will vary.*
1. Readers find Shakespeare difficult not only because of the archaic wording, but also the rearrangement of wording and meter. Shakespeare was meant to be seen and heard—not necessarily read, so by reading the text, difficulties arise. Additionally, Shakespeare wrote his plays for the modern audience—his modern audience, not knowing that his plays would transcend and stand the test of time.
2. Actors would have been available to "fill in" the gaps of the story, and provide a commentary to the text. By reading the text in the classroom, we do not have that support. Although I have read some of Shakespeare's sonnets, I am not familiar with his plays, and am a little worried that I will be able to follow all the action of a full-length play. A student might suggest that the reader do some background reading on Shakespeare and drama, that he might try to see the play, etc.
3. *Ephemeral* means lasting for a short time and leaving no permanent trace. This quality of drama may make a play more difficult to read because a playwright means for his work to be performed live, a situation which adds much of the detail to a play that a playwright includes from the beginning.
4. I am not sure who attends the theater today. I would expect that people who have read Shakespeare's plays or have a lot of money would attend the theater so that they can see one of Shakespeare's plays performed. I would have expected that only rich people attended the theater in Shakespeare's time, but I have learned from the article that both rich and poor people went to the theater and enjoyed Shakespeare all the same.
5. Today, in movie theaters, we have surround sound, reclining theater chairs, cup holders, and a snack stand selling treats at outrageous prices. I am sure that the groundlings who paid a penny to see a play could not have imagined not sitting on the floor, or paying $12 for a small box of popcorn!
6. The lives of actors today are often the object of curiosity and speculation, much like those of Shakespeare's time. Actors today sometimes tend toward a certain kind of role, but not to the extent that one would have during the time of Shakespeare. Modern times have affected the lives of all people, including actors. Due to modern technology, an actor's life can be much more extensively exploited than an actor might have been before. (The student, may, of course, include other ideas so long as they are logical and well thought out.)
7. The four kinds of drama are tragedy, comedy, history, and romance. *Answers will vary.* Most students understand the names for the types of plays in either a more modern or a more literal sense. For instance, many students assume that a comedy will be light-hearted and funny.

Page 30: Shakespeare's Style: The Sonnet Form and Iambic Pentameter
Sonnet will follow ABABCDCDEFEFGG rhyme scheme. Should be divided by syllables. Note: students may have problems with Line 8, thinking it breaks Iambic pentameter and has 11 syllables. (O'er/charged/with/bur/den/of/mine/own/love's/might).

Page 31: Shakespeare's Style: Sonnet Quiz
1. false
2. b. 14
3. true
4. c. rhyming couplet
5. false
6. b. 10 syllables
7. true
8. true
9. Stressed: house, both, like, dig, ty; Unstressed: Two, holds, a, in, ni

Pages 40-41: Act One Scene Guide
Scene Three
Characters: three witches, Macbeth, Banquo, Ross, Angus
Action: Witches appear; meet with Macbeth and Banquo—they give both the prophecies; Ross and Angus tell Macbeth he is the new Thane of Cawdor
Staging: the heath, witches, cauldron
Problem or Solution: Problem—Macbeth and Banquo both want to see how this will play out. Macbeth is already thinking evil thoughts about how he is rising to become king.
Scene Four
Characters: Duncan, Malcolm, Macbeth
Action: Macbeth comes to the King's camp; Duncan thanks him, but names Malcolm his successor. Macbeth is not happy about this.
Staging: same as scene two
Problem or Solution: Problem—Duncan names Malcolm as successor, while Macbeth thought he would be named.
Scene Five
Characters: Lady Macbeth, Macbeth
Action: Lady Macbeth receives Macbeth's letter—she vows to get rid of Duncan, but is afraid Macbeth is not man enough. She asks the gods to make her manly enough to take over if she has to. Macbeth arrives, and they conspire.
Staging: somewhere where Lady Macbeth can be alone with her thoughts—a bedroom or a bathroom? Possibly a library or reading room; Lady Macbeth needs a letter for a prop
Problem or Solution: Problem—Lady Macbeth feels they must kill Duncan, but is Macbeth strong and courageous enough to do it, or will she have to do it herself?
Scene Six
Characters: Duncan, Banquo, Lady Macbeth
Action: Duncan arrives at Macbeth's castle, he feels very comfortable there. Lady Macbeth welcomes him with open arms.
Staging: Outdoors, in the open area of the castle
Problem or Solution: Problem—Duncan feels much too comfortable in Macbeth's castle.
Scene Seven
Characters: Macbeth, Lady Macbeth
Action: Macbeth is having second thoughts about killing Duncan. Lady Macbeth berates him and tries to give him a "pep talk."
Staging: in Macbeth's chamber or a library— somewhere they have privacy

Problem or Solution: Problem—Macbeth is losing his nerve.

Page 42: Act One Comprehension Check
Scene 1
1. after the battle; on the heath; Macbeth
Scene 2
1. Macbeth; he fought and defeated Macdonwald, cutting off his head and carrying it on his sword.
2. Macdonwald
3. Fife; Thane of Cawdor tried to go against Duncan, joining forces with Norway, but Scotland won.
4. Ten thousand dollars; a decent burial of Norway's men
5. Macbeth
Scene 3
1. The first witch asked a fat woman for a chestnut. The woman refused to give her one, so the witches conspire to cause a huge storm while her husband is at sea.
2. They have beards, but they are women.
3. All hail Macbeth, Thane of Glamis, Thane of Cawdor, and King. He is confused because there already is a Thane of Cawdor.
4. lesser than Macbeth, but greater; he shall get kings, but will not be one himself
5. He doesn't know that the Thane of Cawdor was a traitor and removed of his position.
6. to tell Macbeth that he is the new Thane of Cawdor, and to thank Macbeth for his duty
7. He doesn't know that the Thane of Cawdor is going to be executed for treason. Angus tells him he confessed and has been overthrown, and that Macbeth has been named the new Thane of Cawdor.
8. He now has two out of three of the prophecies out of the way (Thane of Glamis, and now Cawdor). The next step is becoming King.
9. The "imperial theme" is becoming King. The two "happy prologues" are becoming Thane of Glamis, then Cawdor.
10. He begins to immediately have bad feelings about the whole thing. He has fears attached to this new position, as the prophecies are unfolding. He decides to let fate take over "If chance will have me king, why, chance may crown me, without my stir." He says he will stay out of the way of his destiny.
Scene 4
1. Cawdor confessed and was executed.
2. Duncan trusted him absolutely.
3. Malcolm
4. He is not happy, and immediately sees Malcolm as a step he must "o'er-leap."
5. He is thinking evil thoughts about getting rid of Malcolm. He wants to kill Malcolm so that he can be king.
Scene 5
1. Macbeth tells Lady all about the witches' prophecies, and how he is now named the Thane of Cawdor, and that next, he will be king, and she will be queen, like she should be.

2. She is thrilled, but is afraid that Macbeth is too much of a sissy and a coward to do what he needs to do in order to make the prophecies come true.

3. She says he is "too full of the milk of human kindness" meaning he is too nice and too wimpy to take matters in his own hands. This is surprising because he was touted and hailed as such a hero in the first few scenes, even having cut off Macdonwald's head.

4. She wants to make everyone feel absolutely welcome. She is planning Duncan's assassination.

5. She wants Macbeth to make sure he puts on a smile and hides what they are about to do to Duncan, so they do not behave suspiciously. If he can pretend everything is fine, she plans to take care of all the rest.

Scene 6
1. He is feeling very, very comfortable and welcome. It is ironic that he feels so welcome and safe, since this is where he will have his guard down and be killed.

Scene 7
1. Duncan's murder

2. He knows he trusts him as a kinsmen (he is a cousin) and a citizen/soldier. He actually likes Duncan and respects him, and feels as if he is really betraying him.

3. He feels as if he has been honored by Duncan lately, and that he is beginning to be respected and admired by everyone.

4. She is irate, and calls him something less than a man.

5. She is saying that by him calling off the murder, it is like nursing a newborn, who is trusting and comfortable in one's arms, then pulling away the nipple and bashing in his face. She compares this to what Macbeth is doing to her—teasing her with this great news, then "bashing" it by changing his mind. She is a drama-queen, and is hoping to manipulate Macbeth. She has to get his attention, so her dramatics are probably the way she often gets her way.

6. She says that if they fail, they fail, but if he doesn't give up, and if he does what she tells him, they won't fail.

7. The plan is to get everyone drunk, then sneak in to Duncan's room, kill him, then plant the daggers on the drunk guards, who won't know what happened.

8. *Answers will vary.* Lady Macbeth certainly manipulates Macbeth, so no wonder she sees him as a coward and a sissy. She seems to have a flair for the dramatic, and knows how to work Macbeth to get what she wants. One loses respect for Macbeth when he is around his wife, which is not what we expected of him in the previous scenes.

9. Yes, they did seem legitimate, since he tried to back out of the plan, then he was not able to stand up to her. At this point, it looks like Lady Macbeth may have to murder Duncan herself.

Pages 44-45: Act One Standards Focus: Dialogue, Monologue, and More
Part A
1. Scene 3; lines 52-61
   a. monologue
   b. Banquo wants to know what the witches predict for him, since they have given Macbeth such intriguing prophecies.
2. Scene 3; lines 127-137
   a. asides
   b. we as the audience are hearing Macbeth's inner thoughts. He is already having some deep and dark thoughts about the prophecies and his instincts tell him something is wrong.
3. Scene 5
   a. stage direction
   b. Lady Macbeth gets the letter from Macbeth and learns about the witches' prophecies. The director knows that Lady Macbeth must be somewhere alone to read the letter.
4. Scene 5, lines 37-42
   a. soliloquy
   b. Lady Macbeth is alone with her thoughts. We learn how evil her thoughts are and how unnatural she is. She wants to be like a man so that she can direct her husband to murder Duncan, or if he is unable, to do it herself.
5. Scene 5; lines 58-60
   a. dialogue
   b. Lady Macbeth tells Macbeth that she wants to kill Duncan, which has not even occurred to Macbeth at this point.

Part B
Answers will vary widely.

Part C
Answers will vary. Sample student answers are given.
1. Shakespeare clearly wanted the audience to be involved in the action of the play. By writing in so many asides, we can learn about everyone's state of mind, especially Macbeth's. These asides add a sense of excitement, involvement, and suspense, as the audience learns more about each character and how their minds work.

2. Monologues are long speeches within a play. Soliloquies are long speeches given by a character when he or she is alone or thinks he or she is alone. These are the character's inner thoughts spoken aloud.

3. I think that the real value of Shakespeare's play is in the words that are spoken. When a character absolutely needs stage directions, they are either given as stage direction, or they can be found in the words the characters speak. It is up to the director and the actors to interpret how and when a character would naturally move, given the spoken text.

4. A soliloquy is a long speech given by a character when he or she is alone or thinks he or she is alone on stage. These are the character's inner thoughts spoken aloud. In an aside, a character is speaking so that the audience can hear, but the character knows he/she is not alone on stage. The character

may still think his or her inner thoughts, but there is still an awareness of the other characters onstage.

Pages 47-48: Act One Standards Focus: Mood
List of moods will vary. For a comprehensive list, please visit our blog at secondarysolutionsblog.com.
Part A
Answers will vary. Sample answers are given.
1. *Underlined*: brave, Fortune, brandished steel, smoked, bloody executions, valor's minion, faced the slave
    Moods: brave, courageous, hostile, fearless
2. *Underlined:* good, horrid, unfix my hair, heart knock, against, nature
    Moods: fear, trepidation, anxiety
3. *Underlined:* worthiest, sin, ingratitude, heavy, recompense, slow
    Moods: regret, sorrow, distress
4. *Underlined:* hide, fires, black, deep desires, fears
    Moods: fear, revenge, willpower, evil
5. *Underlined:* spirits, mortal, unsex, crown, direst cruelty
    Moods: evil, unnatural, insane, foreboding
6. *Underlined:* pleasant, nimbly, sweetly, gentle senses
    Moods: happy, comfortable, airy, light, welcoming

Part B
1. There seems to be a dark and foreboding sense of evil and unnaturalness throughout the majority of Act One.
2. The witches make the predictions for Macbeth, Macbeth accepts his fate, but then thinks evil thoughts when Malcolm is appointed. Lady Macbeth receives Macbeth's letter and only thinks of murdering Duncan so that Macbeth can be king.
3. The moods are changed when Macbeth is hailed as a hero in Scene 2—we begin to respect him. The mood goes back to dark and sinister until Duncan arrives at Inverness, and he feels comfortable and safe. Again, the mood changes back after that to an evil and dark mood. He does this by changing the words to match the mood he wants to portray. The characters use powerful vocabulary to express themselves, and the moods reflect the use of great words arranged with great imagery or figurative language. To me, the changes in mood add great suspense. The "light" parts of the play so far are few and far between. This gives me the impression that everything will get really dark and evil as the rest of the play unfolds.

Pages 49-52 Act One Assessment Preparation: Context Clues
Part A
For b. Synonym based on Inference, and for d. Explanation will vary. Sample student answers are given.

1. Captain
    a. noun
    b. sword
    c. n. submissive follower or dependent
    d. By the word "carved" I thought it might be a weapon like a knife or sword.
2. First Witch
    a. verb
    b. shrink
    c. v. to make or become gradually less
    d. I have seen this word before.
3. Banquo
    a. adjective
    b. old
    c. adj. dried up or shriveled
    d. I thought it meant old because the witches look old.
4. Macbeth
    a. adjective
    b. visionary
    c. adj. of, or a characteristic of, a prophet or prophecy
    d. Since the witches made a prediction or prophecy, I was able to guess that the word was related and that the greeting was also prophetic.
5. Banquo
    a. noun
    b. problems
    c. n. things of little importance or value
    d. I thought he was referring to the problems that were being introduced by the witches' prophecies.
6. Macbeth
    a. noun
    b. doubt
    c. v. to infer with little evidence; n. an idea or opinion based on little evidence.
    d. I assumed since "nothing is but what is not" is there, that there was some doubt or second-guessing going on.

Part B
For b. Explanation will vary.
1. a. n. a period between two events; b. I don't think there is anything here that helps make the word understandable.
2. a. v. appealed to; asked; b. I can infer from the idea that he is asking for a pardon that the word implored has something to do with asking.
3. a. n. ungratefulness; b. To show gratitude means to be grateful. In=not.
4. a. n. a forerunner of what is to come; b. This one may be able to figure out by the fact that Macbeth says his he is going to leave and tell his wife of the approach, but that is a stretch.
5. a. v. to criticize severely; b. There is not much here to support the word in the way of context clues.
6. a. adj. deserving of shame, deeply wrong; b. This is not a well-used or common word, and the context clues do not really help, but we know she is up to evil thoughts!

7. a. n. decorated cup; b. By taking something poisonous to "our own lips" we may be able to assume it is a poisoned drink of some sort.
8. a. adj. strength, determination; b. These lines do not give clues to the meaning.

Pages 53-54: Act Two Scene Guide
Scene One
Characters: Banquo, Macbeth, Lady Macbeth, Porter, Macduff, Lennox, Malcolm, Donalbain
Action: Banquo gives Macbeth a diamond ring for Lady Macbeth from Duncan; they talk about Banquo's nightmares about the witches. Macbeth sees a vision of a bloody dagger leading him to kill Duncan.
Staging: bloody dagger "floating" as Macbeth's vision
Problem or Solution: Problem—Macbeth is going to kill Duncan, and he feels he is being led by outside forces to do it.
Scene Two
Characters: Lady Macbeth and Macbeth
Action: Lady Macbeth drugged the men, then Lady and Macbeth meet. Macbeth is disturbed by what he did, and he forgot to plant the daggers. Lady Macbeth grabs them and plants them herself.
Staging: Macbeth must have bloodied hands, holding daggers. Lady must grab the daggers, then upon re-entering, have bloody hands herself.
Problem or Solution: Solution—Lady Macbeth has successfully planted the daggers, and all is going according to plan. Now they wait.
Scene Three
Characters: Porter, Macduff, Lennox, Malcolm, Donalbain, Macbeth, Lady Macbeth
Action: There is a knocking at the door, and the Porter answers. Macduff and Lennox have arrived to wake the king. Macduff finds the king dead. Macbeth and Lady act like they don't know what is going on. Malcolm and Donalbain arrive, and fear that they are next. Malcolm decides to flee to England, while Donalbain decides to go to Ireland.
Staging: The Porter needs to have a door to let Macduff and Lennox in.
Problem or Solution: both—this scene can be considered a solution, since to Lady Macbeth and Macbeth, their "problem" of Duncan and becoming King has been solved. However, it creates more problems, as questions arise of who did it, and why.
Scene Four
Characters: Ross, old Man
Action: Ross and the old Man discuss how unnatural things have been happening—dark during the day, horses eating each other
Staging: outside the castle
Problem or Solution: Problem—things are not good, and the universe and nature are reflecting that

Pages 55-56: Act Two Comprehension Check
Scene One
1. After midnight
2. He keeps having nightmares about the witches.
3. A diamond. He was in an unusually great mood, and very content.

4. that he never thinks of the witches or their predictions
5. a bloody dagger leading him to the king's chamber
6. He says "wicked dreams abuse the curtain'd sleep"
7. that the men have been drugged and they are now passed out in the king's chamber; it is now time for Macbeth to kill the king
Scene Two
1. She has been drinking as well, but it is making her "bold" and strong to do what she has to do.
2. He looked like her father.
3. One of the men laughed, and another yelled "murder"; they woke each other up, but fell asleep again.
4. He thinks he hears a voice say "Sleep no more! Macbeth does murder sleep." It is his guilty conscience getting to him.
5. He forgot to plant the daggers on the men.
6. She grabs the daggers and does it herself.
7. All the blood everywhere.
8. She assumes that if the blood is gone from their hands, there will be no evidence of the murder, and they will go on happily with their plan. She does not take into account the feelings associated with the deed. It is not easy to kill someone, and wash your hands of the entire thing, unless you are a psychopath.
9. "Wake Duncan with thy knocking! I would thou couldst!"
Scene Three
1. The audience has just witnessed Duncan's murder, and all the anxiety and fear Macbeth is feeling. The audience needs a break from the blood and darkness.
2. Macbeth's castle is turning into a hell, as Duncan is murdered, and Macbeth and Lady Macbeth could go to hell for their evil deeds.
3. Alcohol makes people act rudely, boldly, and vulgarly. He talks about how alcohol makes men have the desire for sex, but also makes them unable to perform sexually.
4. He has come to wake the king, upon his command.
5. Lennox says that the earth shook, chimneys were blown down, screams of death were heard, and birds made noise all night long.
6. Macduff
7. He confesses that he killed the king's men because he saw evidence that they had killed the king.
8. She faints; she could be faking, wanting to distract everyone from what her husband just said, or she could be really overwhelmed, as Macbeth acted against the plan, and she is truly disturbed by what he did.
9. Malcolm goes to England; Donalbain to Ireland; They don't trust the men around the king—and fear they are next to be murdered.
Scene Four
1. Ross and the old Man discuss how unnatural things have been happening—dark during the day, horses eating each other, hawk killed by a mousing

owl, horses broke out of their stalls against their men

2. Malcolm and Donalbain, because they ran away so quickly after the murder.

Pages 57-58: Act Two Standards Focus: Figurative Language

1. a. metaphor; b. the seeds of time are a metaphor for looking into the future, and seeing what will happen in the future.
2. a. personification; b. chance, or fate, is personified with giving the crown to Macbeth to become king
3. a. personification; b. time and the hour are personified to "run" through the rough day; time goes on
4. a. hyperbole; b. in this case, Macbeth has done so much, that Duncan can never repay him.
5. A) a. personification; b. knife has eyes to see the wound, B) a. personification; b. heaven has eyes to "peep" through, C) a. metaphor; b. the dark is thick and envelops like a blanket
6. a. personification; b. the intent is able to trip over itself and fall, like a set of clumsy feet
7. a. simile; b. the summons is very heavy, like lead, showing its importance
8. a. personification; b. sleep is a tangible entity, like a person, who can be murdered.
9. a. hyperbole; b. Macbeth feels there is so much blood, not even the entire ocean has enough water to get rid of it.
10. a. personification; b. murder is as a burglar, who is able to break into the temple and steal the life (Duncan)

Pages 59-61: Act Two Standards Focus: Plot and Conflict
Part A

1. The Captain tells King Duncan how bravely and nobly Macbeth fought Macdonwald.
2. The Witches tell Macbeth that he will become Thane of Cawdor and king.
3. King Duncan announces that Macbeth will be the new Thane of Cawdor.
4. The King announces Malcolm will become the King's successor.
5. Lady Macbeth learns about the witches' prophecies.
6. Macbeth sees the imaginary dagger leading him to kill the king.
7. Lady Macbeth drugs Duncan's servants.
8. Macbeth murders Duncan.
9. Lady Macbeth takes the daggers to place them on the king's men and hide her husband's deed.
10. Macduff finds the murdered king.
11. Macbeth tells everyone that he killed the king's men for what they had done.
12. Duncan's sons flee, and are blamed for the king's murder.
13. Macbeth is to be named the new King of Scotland.

Part B

1. a. Macbeth versus himself; b. man versus himself; c. Macbeth doesn't get how he will be able to become Thane of Cawdor, since there already is one, let alone king.
2. a. Lady Macbeth versus Macbeth; b. man versus man; c. Lady Macbeth has no faith in Macbeth and sees him as a complete sissy. She feels that if he can't do the deed, she will have to do it herself.
3. a. Macbeth versus himself; b. man versus himself; c. Macbeth is having a major inner struggle finding the strength to kill Duncan, since he likes him and respects him.
4. a. Macbeth versus Lady Macbeth; b. man versus man; c. Lady Macbeth continues to fight against Macbeth's better judgment, although Macbeth tends to weaken around his wife.
5. a. Macbeth versus himself; b. man versus himself; c. Macbeth is horrified by what he has done, and now begins to regret his actions.

Page 62: Act Two Assessment Preparation: Word Usage

1. allegiance
2. carousing—having fun; lamenting—feeling and acting depressed and sad
3. scruples
4. augment
5. quenched
6. a gold statue; a gold picture frame
7. kicking or teasing it
8. malice
9. dire situation—really bad—deadly
10. immaterial, doubtful, ethereal
11. having a conversation
12. predominance
13. summons
14. clamored

Pages 63-64: Act Three Scene Guide
Scene One
Characters: Banquo, Macbeth, Lady Macbeth, two murderers
Action: Banquo suspects Macbeth of Duncan's murder; Macbeth fears Banquo, turns to murderers to murder Banquo and Fleance
Staging: a room in the palace—no specific props
Problem or Solution: Problem—Macbeth begins to let his fears and ambition get the best of him, killing anyone in his way.
Scene Two
Characters: Lady Macbeth, Macbeth
Action: Lady Macbeth is beginning to feel guilty, and she expresses this to Macbeth. Macbeth hints at Banquo's murder, but won't tell Lady Macbeth about his plans.
Staging: a room in the palace—no specific props
Problem or Solution: Problem—Lady Macbeth is beginning to feel overwhelmed with guilt
Scene Three
Characters: three murderers, Banquo, Fleance

Action: Murderers ambush Banquo and Fleance; Banquo is killed, but Fleance flees
Staging: outside; bushes and/or trees to hide the murderers
Problem or Solution: Problem—Fleance has escaped; Banquo is dead because of Macbeth, and Macbeth's power increases.

Scene Four
Characters: Macbeth, Murderer, Lady Macbeth
Action: Macbeth finds out that Banquo was murdered, but that Fleance escaped. Macbeth sees Banquo's ghost at the table—he becomes hysterical. Lady Macbeth tries to say it was from childhood seizures, but as Macbeth begins to say too much, Lady Macbeth tells everyone to go home.
Staging: great feast in the palace; Banquo's ghost
Problem or Solution: Problem—Macbeth's conscience is getting to him; he may be losing his mind.

Scene Five
Characters: three witches, Hecate
Action: Hecate is mad that she wasn't able to show her abilities by helping with Macbeth.
Staging: forest or heath, witches cauldron
Problem or Solution: neither

Scene Six
Characters: Lennox and another Lord
Action: Lennox and the other Lord give exposition about Banquo's murder, Fleance's escape, and Macduff's refusal to attend the feast, and Macduff joining Malcolm and Siward in England to ask for help getting rid of Macbeth.
Staging: nothing specific
Problem or Solution: Solution—finally someone will be rising up against Macbeth

Pages 65-66 Act Three: Comprehension Check
Scene One
1. Finally, we see that Banquo suspects Macbeth of murdering Duncan.
2. He hopes that his prophecies will come true as well.
3. That they are in England and Ireland, not confessing, but telling everyone lies of some kind.
4. He wants Banquo murdered because he sees him as a threat. He doesn't want him to get in his way during his rule as king, but also, he doesn't want Banquo's prophecy coming true as Banquo's children are predicted to take the throne.
5. He is afraid it would look bad to their common friends.
6. That night, while they are out for a ride, before the banquet.
7. He should be afraid of Banquo—Banquo is suspicious of him, and although right now he is loyal, he may turn on him, and he has the power to turn others against Macbeth too.

Scene Two
1. She says "Naught's had, all's spent, Where our desire is got without content." She is not content with where she is. She thought she would be happier, and wonders if it is how she got to the throne (by killing Duncan to get there) is what is ruining it for her.
2. She thinks he is too caught up in his thoughts and troubles.
3. Macbeth basically says "Don't worry your pretty little head about these little things, until you find out what I've done, and can applaud me for it.

Scene Three
1. Fleance escaped.
2. *Answers will vary widely. Accept all reasonably supported responses.*

Scene Four
1. He says basically that he is more afraid than ever.
2. Because he is seeing Banquo's ghost could be an indication that Macbeth is beginning to really slip from reality. He could be becoming insane.
3. That he has a medical problem (seizures) from childhood.
4. She tells him it is not real, but his imagination. She also tries to tell him that ghosts are an old wives' tale.
5. This is Macbeth slipping into insanity. He is seeing the ghost of Banquo because his conscience is getting to him. He is the only one who can see him because it is a problem in Macbeth's head and not a reality.
6. Macduff
7. *Answers will vary. Accept all reasonable responses.*

Scene Five
1. It may have been added as a break to the audience, since they have just witnessed Macbeth possibly slipping into insanity. It could also have been a scene so that the stagehands could disassemble any fancy staging or lighting that made Banquo's ghost appear.
2. She wanted to "play" by showing off what she could do to Macbeth.
3. Macbeth is coming.
4. Hecate is saying that one should be on guard if one becomes too comfortable. (Reminds the audience of Duncan and his fate.) *Answers will vary.*
5. *Answers will vary. Accept all reasonable responses.*

Scene Six
1. that Duncan was pitied of Macbeth, then he was dead; that Banquo wound up dead; Fleance might as well have been killed, as he has fled; and Malcolm and Donalbain killed their father
2. They have been rallying the troops of England with Siward to overthrow Macbeth.

Pages 67-68: Act Three Standards Focus: Irony
1. He shouldn't have trusted Macbeth because he was planning to murder him
2. With all the evil going on (Duncan's murder) it is like hell, also Lady Macbeth and Macbeth will probably go to hell because of their deeds.
3. The weird sisters never said anything about Banquo being a problem for Macbeth—it was just his pure greed to be king forever.

4. Lennox is being sarcastic. He knows Macbeth is to blame and that it didn't grieve him because he did it.
5. He is able to see the ghost because he killed him and he is being haunted because of it. It could also be his guilty conscience causing visions.
6. She may be starting to feel a little guilty about how she became queen, as she should.
7. Macbeth plans to murder Banquo and Fleance that day. He is very pleasant with him, but is really plotting to murder him.
8. Macbeth knows why Banquo isn't there—because he had him murdered that afternoon.
9. It develops a special enjoyment and interest for the reader/audience as he/she feels like they are a part of the action of the play, and that they are "in" on the secrets going on. We are able to see potential problems before the characters do, and so we are able to enjoy or fear their process of discovery.

Pages 69-71: Act Three Standards Focus: Characterization
Part One
1. a. Duncan is very trusting; b. Duncan trusted the former Thane of Cawdor, who turned out to be a traitor, then trusted Macbeth, who killed him.
2. a. Lady Macbeth is conniving and manipulative; b. She is the one who convinces Macbeth to kill Duncan even though he didn't even want to and had second thoughts about it.
3. a. He feels extremely guilty about killing Duncan. b. He feels he will never be able to wash his hands clean, nor clear his conscience for what he has done—it will haunt him forever.
4. a. Banquo is hopeful. b. He is hopeful that his prophecies will come true, just as Macbeth's have. He wonders how it will all come to pass.

Part Two
1. a. Macbeth is brave and a hero. b. This is at the beginning of the play and serves to build Macbeth up for his tragic downfall.
2. a. They are ugly and look like withered old men. b. They are "other-worldy" and should not be listened to—let alone trusted to tell the truth.
3. a. Lady Macbeth doesn't respect her husband and thinks more of herself. b. She is the one to plant the daggers after Macbeth fails to do so.

Page 72: Act Three Assessment Preparation: Vocabulary Builders
Answers will vary widely.

Page 73: Act Four Scene Guide
Scene One
Characters: three witches, Hecate, Macbeth, apparitions
Action: Witches are making a potion; Macbeth wants to know more about his future; apparitions appear to tell him his future in riddle; Macbeth finds out Macduff went to England
Staging: cave, cauldron

Problem or Solution: Problem—Macbeth is becoming more obsessed with knowing more, and getting deeper into his insanity. He plans to kill Macduff and his family.
Scene Two
Characters: Ross, Lady Macduff, Macduff's son, Messenger, murderers
Action: Ross tells Lady Macduff that Macduff left for England; She is mad, and calls him a traitor; Messenger warns them to leave—she refuses. The Murderers arrive and kill everyone.
Staging: a kitchen or a living area
Problem or Solution: Problem—Macbeth is only causing more problems by now killing innocent people.
Scene Three
Characters: Malcolm, Macduff, Ross
Action: Malcolm and Macduff discuss the problems in Scotland. Malcolm is suspicious, so he tests Macduff by saying what an awful ruler he would be if he were in charge. Macduff passes the test, and they agree to join forces. Ross arrives to tell Macduff that his family is dead. Macduff vows revenge.
Staging: nothing in particular. Maybe chairs?
Problem or Solution: Solution—they are going to finally try to overthrow Macbeth.

Page 74: Act Four Comprehension Check
Scene One
1. An armed head—Beware Macduff
2. A bloody child—None of woman born shall harm Macbeth; he knows Macduff was born of woman, so he feels he doesn't need to fear Macduff, and can ignore the first apparition's warning
3. A crowned child with a tree in hand—Macbeth will never be killed until Birnam Wood comes to Dunsinane. He says there is no way the woods can move to Dunsinane, and dismisses the warning.
4. He wants to know if Banquo's children will one day rule in the kingdom. The witches show him a long line of men with one at the end who is holding a mirror. All the men look like Banquo.
5. It is ironic because he is cursing himself—he has trusted the witches, and will be damned because of it.
6. England; to kill his family and everyone dear to Macduff
Scene Two
1. She is not happy, and argues with Ross.
2. Ross says that there is a good reason Macduff has left, although he cannot talk about it.
3. She says he is a traitor.
4. That she will easily find herself a new husband, since Macduff has only left and is not dead.
5. She doesn't feel she should leave her home. She doesn't want to leave.
Scene Three
1. There has been too much going on for Malcolm to trust anyone. He is wise to not just trust Macduff right away, considering Duncan, his father, trusted too many people too fully and paid the ultimate price for it.

2. a tyrant; they are disgusted and ashamed to call Scotland their home

3. Malcolm acts like he, too, is a lecher and a tyrant. He talks about how he would run the country into the ground.

4. He would take advantage of all the women, to fill the "cistern" of his lust; he would steal the landowners' money and turn the people against each other so that he could reap the rewards of them killing each other.

5. Siward; they have already gathered 10,000 men, ready to fight at a moment's notice

6. He says that King Edward can cure people with prayer and that he has the gift of prophecy.

7. He tells Macduff that Macbeth had his family murdered. He is overwhelmed, shocked, and upset. He realizes that it was all his own fault because he left them to go to England.

8. He vows to get revenge against Macbeth, in the name of all those close to him.

Pages 75-76: Act Four Standards Focus: Character Analysis
Macbeth
Internal: After he murders Duncan, he feels terribly guilty and wishes he could take it back. From there, he continues his ascent into evil, acting on his whims and killing anyone he perceives to be in his way.
External: Macbeth versus Lady Macbeth, Macbeth versus Macduff
Influences: the witches, Lady Macbeth, his own ambition, his conscience, the apparitions
Lady Macbeth
Main
Internal: Her avarice, then guilt about Duncan's murder and Macbeth's decline into evil; her feelings that she gained her position as queen wrongly; her conscience
External: Macbeth
Main Motive: to help her husband to become king so she can be queen
Influence: herself, Macbeth at times
Macduff
Main
Internal: his suspicions about Macbeth; his grief over his family
External: Macbeth versus Macduff
Main Motive: to remove Macbeth from power and gain revenge
Influence: his own suspicions, Malcolm, the death of his family

Pages 77-78: Act Four Standards Focus: Motif
Examples may vary, as there can be many.
1. Blood
   a. Bloody soldier telling about Macbeth's courageousness (Act 1, Sc. 2)
   b. Bloody dagger leading Macbeth (Act. 2, Sc. 1)
   c. Blood on Macbeth and Lady Macbeth's hands after Duncan's murder (Act 2, Sc. 2)
   d. There is a lot of blood in the play, since there is a lot of murder and evil going on. The graphic nature of all the blood really helps the audience to appreciate the depth of the situation in a visual way.

2. Sleep
   a. Duncan rests easy and comfortably at Macbeth's castle, unaware of what is coming (Act 2, Sc. 1)
   b. Macbeth is having nightmares about the witches. (Act 2, Sc. 2)
   c. "Macbeth does murder sleep" (Act 2, Sc.2)
   d. Sleep, or the lack of it, is mentioned several times throughout the play. In sleep, we dream, which many say is a reflection of our subconscious. Sleep is also considered a temporary or "mini" death to some.

3. Reversal of Nature
   a. Lady Macbeth exclaims "unsex me here," asking to become a man (Act 1, Sc. 5)
   b. Malcolm and Donalbain are suspected of murdering their own father—an unimaginable deed. (Act 2, Sc. 2)
   c. Ross and the old Man talk about the horses eating each other. and the mousing owl attacking the hawk. (Act 2, Sc. 4)
   d. The evil things that are happening can be seen as a disturbance in the way the world is supposed to work. Macbeth has messed with fate and nature is striking back.

4. Visions/Hallucinations/Supernatural Elements
   a. Macbeth speaks to the witches, Act 1, Scene 2
   b. Macbeth sees the bloody dagger leading him to kill Duncan, Act 2, Sc. 1
   c. Macbeth sees Banquo's ghost at the banquet, Act 3, Sc. 4
   d. Visions and hallucinations can be seen as a reflection of one's conscience—and in this case, Macbeth's guilt getting to him. The supernatural element adds a feeling that forces beyond nature are in control. The three together give the play deeper meaning, as Macbeth seems to embrace the forces of evil or the unnatural.

5. Darkness and Night
   a. "Let not light see my black and deep desires" Macbeth says upon learning about Malcolm's claim to the throne. (Act 1, Sc. 4)
   b. Lady Macbeth asks that the "dunnest smoke of hell" hide the deeds and "nor heaven peep through the blanket of the dark." (Act 1, Sc. 5)
   c. "By the clock 'tis day, and yet dark night strangles the travelling lamp." (Act. 2, Sc. 2)
   d. Darkness and night is often associated with evil and the "dark side." The more darkness that is seen or mentioned, the darker the play becomes, paralleling Macbeth's decline.

Page 79: Act Four Assessment Preparation: Vocabulary Extension
1. desolate
2. sovereignty
3. teems
4. pernicious

5. cistern
6. resolute
7. quarry
8. entrails
9. relish
10. laudable
11. antic
12. dolor
13. bodements
14. malady
15. avaricious

Pages 80-81 Act Five Scene Guide
Scene One
Characters: Doctor, Lady Macbeth's attendant, Lady Macbeth
Action: Lady Macbeth is sleepwalking and washing her hands. The Doctor and her attendant watch and discuss.
Staging: Lady Macbeth must have a light near her.
Problem or Solution: Problem—Lady Macbeth has slipped fully into insanity, and now she is a danger to herself.
Scene Two
Characters: Mentieth, Caithness, Angus, Lennox
Action: The men gather the troops, discussing how Macbeth is getting ready for attack.
Staging: none in particular
Problem or Solution: neither OR beginning of Solution, as Macbeth will soon be facing his demise
Scene Three
Characters: Macbeth, Doctor, Seyton
Action: Macbeth still clings to hope that the prophecies are true, but calls for his armor in order to fight. The doctor tells Macbeth about Lady Macbeth's "disease."
Scene Four
Characters: Malcolm, Mentieth, Siward, Macduff
Action: Malcolm orders the men to cut down part of a tree to disguise themselves moving closer to Dunsinane.
Staging: lots of soldiers with branches
Problem or Solution: Solution—By the soldiers holding the branches of Birnam Wood, they will ascend on Dunsinane, making the third apparition's words come true
Scene Five
Characters: Macbeth, Seyton
Action: Macbeth learns that Lady Macbeth is dead; a messenger announces Birnam Wood is coming. Macbeth vows to die fighting.
Staging: Inside the castle, flags of Scotland
Problem or Solution: Solution—Lady Macbeth is now dead, seemingly out of her misery. Macbeth braces himself for attack.
Scene Six
Characters: Malcolm, Siward
Action: The soldiers continue to advance, now without the branches.
Staging: men should be tattered from fighting, should have weapons
Problem or Solution: neither

Scene Seven
Characters: Macbeth, Young Siward, Macduff
Action: Macbeth kills Young Siward and feels temporarily better; Macduff shows up
Staging: men in armor
Problem or Solution: Solution—Macbeth feels comforted knowing that Young Siward was not able to kill him
Scene Eight
Characters: Macbeth, Macbeth, Siward, Malcolm
Action: Maduff fights with and kills Macbeth, later enters with his head on his sword; Siward learns his son was killed; they declare victory and head off to crown Malcolm king.
Staging: Macbeth's head on Macduff's sword
Problem or Solution: Solution—Macbeth the tyrant is finally dead and now Malcolm can be king.

Page 82: Act Five Comprehension Check
Scene One
1. Lady Macbeth has been sleepwalking.
2. She has been trying to wash her hands. She says "out, damned spot." She is trying to get the blood off her hands.
3. He says she needs divine intervention, and tells her attendant to remove anything she could use to hurt herself.
Scene Two
1. Mentieth, Caithness, Angus, Lennox
2. He has strongly fortified Dunsinane, and is ready for the fight.
Scene Three
1. He is thinking about the apparitions and what they said about Birnam Wood and "none of woman born." He tries to convince himself that there is no possible way either could ever be true.
2. that 10,000 men are approaching
3. He wants Seyton to grab his armor and get him ready to fight.
4. He tells the Doctor to give her whatever medicine she needs; the Doctor says there is no medicine to cure her.
Scene Four
1. Malcolm tells the men to disguise themselves with the branches of the trees of Birnam Wood. This is how the prophecy will pan out.
Scene Five
1. He is dismissive, and basically says "that's life!"
2. Macbeth is talking about our time on this earth. We are all here for such little time on the earth, and the time we are here is insignificant. He is basically saying that life is nothing important, and that our brief time on this earth means nothing.
3. That Birnam Wood is moving to Dunsinane. Macbeth never thought this would be possible—now the prophecies are coming true.
Scene Seven
1. Young Siward—he was able to kill him so the "none of woman born" prophecy was not coming true—or so he thought.
2. Macduff

Scene Eight

1. He feels he has spilled too much of his blood already by killing his family.
2. He was not delivered vaginally.
3. He does not back down, but fights to the death.
4. That Young Siward was killed.
5. Macbeth's head
6. Malcolm; they predicted one of Banquo's sons would be king
7. *Answers will vary.*

Page 84: Act Five Standards Focus: Tragedy and the Tragic Hero

Answers may vary.

1. His tragic flaw is his ambition and the total and complete disregard for the natural way things work.
2. He seems happy. He feels respected as a soldier, and even mentions that, when he is hesitant about killing Duncan. He tries to convince his wife that he is gaining the respect he wants.
3. He has a high title, and gets promoted, and is a war hero.
4. I believe Macbeth was a moral and ethical person who had too much presented to him, and therefore he got greedy and too ambitious. He had the second thoughts about believing the witches, and he had second thoughts about not killing Duncan, but he was too wimpy and listened to everyone around him, rather than himself.
5. There might be two places where Macbeth really sees what he has done. First, right after he kills Duncan and was too disturbed to place the daggers, and second, when he hears that Macduff was not born of woman. Even though he goes on to ignore his guilt, we definitely witness his feelings as he even says that he wishes Duncan were still alive. However, we do not see any of this guilt later, until the very end, when he still feels he is safe—until he learns of Macduff's birth. This is not consistent with the tragic hero for two reasons: first, he has his epiphany early on, but ignores it. Second, we never witness his catharsis, since the fighting and actual death take place off-stage.
6. I do not believe Macbeth was the ideal tragic hero because there were too many external forces intervening in his demise. Had he done all these things on his own, without the push of the witches or his wife, I would have had an easier time accepting his fall from grace as his own. He is ruled by external forces and ignores his inner motivation or strength, which ultimately causes his downfall.
7. Yes, *Macbeth* is truly a tragedy, according to the definition. Throughout the play we fear and pity both Macbeth and Lady Macbeth as we are taken on a rollercoaster of their deeds. We may even feel sorry that Macbeth has been so manipulated by the witches and his wife, when it seemed so unnecessary. I did not feel a catharsis because the killing and everything is so far removed from my own life. I felt better knowing that everything was over and that Macbeth was finally out of power, but it was not something I related to my own life.

Pages 85-87: Act Five Standards Focus: Theme Part One

Answers will vary. Accept all reasonable responses.

1. Theme: Ambition
   a. "The Prince of Cumberland! That is a step On which I must fall down, or else o'erleap, For in my way it lies." Macbeth
   b. Macbeth has just learned Malcolm will succeed Duncan.
   c. Act One, Scene 4
   d. This is the beginning of Macbeth truly thinking evil thoughts to get rid of something in the way of his goals.
2. Theme: Guilt
   a. "Will all great Neptune's ocean wash this blood Clean from my hand? No, this my hand will rather The multitudinous seas incarnadine, Making the green one red." Macbeth
   b. Macbeth sees his hands covered with Duncan's blood and immediately is plagued by the guilt of his deed.
   c. Act Two, Scene 2
   d. Hands covered in blood are symbolic of guilt in this play, as Macbeth breaks down in this scene, and Lady Macbeth tries to wash her bloody hands in Act Five.
3. Theme: Trust versus Betrayal
   a. "He's here in double trust: First, as I am his kinsman and his subject, Strong both against the deed; then, as his host, Who should against his murderer shut the door, Not bear the knife myself." Macbeth
   b. Macbeth has second thoughts about killing Duncan.
   c. Act One, Scene 7
   d. Duncan was far too trusting of everyone, and he was betrayed. Macbeth took advantage of that trust, although he recognized it. The theme could be "Be careful who you trust."
4. Theme: Fate versus Free Will
   a. "If chance will have me king, why, chance may crown me without my stir" Macbeth
   b. Macbeth has just heard the witches predictions, and he vows to stay out of the way and let fate happen.
   c. Act One, Scene 3
   d. This is important because although Macbeth has said that he will not get involved in the plan that fate has for him, all he does is get involved and try to manipulate his fate.
5. Theme: Nature versus the Unnatural
   a. "By the clock 'tis day, And yet dark night strangles the travelling lamp" Ross

b. Right after Duncan's murder, the world doesn't seem right. It should be day, but it is dark as night.

c. Act Two, Scene 4

d. The world seems to be turning upside down, as nature is reflecting the evil that is beginning to pervade the play.

Part Two

Answers will vary. Accept all reasonable responses.

1. Animal Farm also has this theme. Because the animals blindly believed everything Napoleon said and did to be right, his actions went unchecked, and he became a tyrant. This can also be seen in the case of Hitler, whose uncontrolled power took over and contributed to World War II.

2. I completely believe this to be true. Teenagers are especially susceptible to this via peer pressure. Even though they know the right thing to do, they ignore their conscience and morals and follow the crowd.

3. There has to be a point to a story. We want to know that there is a reason for reading and we like to follow as people learn important lessons, and by that, we live vicariously through these characters.

4. I feel the most important theme is "Be careful who you trust." Duncan was too trusting of everyone, which caused his death, and Macbeth was too trusting of what he heard from the witches.

Page 88: Act Five Assessment Preparation: Vocabulary in Context

1. separating the people; listen to both sides, let them take turns speaking

2. rude people, bad drivers, and the toilet seat left up

3. you are being chastised, scolded—you are in trouble

4. After he confessed, he was condemned to death.

5. When Malcolm was named Duncan's successor; when he felt Banquo was in his way of remaining king

6. More—pristine is very excellent condition

7. so that it wouldn't be easily broken

8. close relationship with God, very religious, have a lot of money, live in a good house, have lots of close friends, be in good health

9. because they think they don't understand how a teenager feels, or teens think parents don't trust them

10. someone may have spread an untrue rumor about me

11. ignore him, move to the next room; tell my mom

12. it might be getting ready to strike with all its force

13. possibly the rich, politicians, or maybe celebrities

14. it will burst all over you

15. lots of plants, mud, overhanging trees, dirt

Pages 90-91: Act One Quiz

1. h. If chance wants him to be king" chance will crown" him.

2. b. comes up with the plan to assassinate the king

3. a. will never be king, but will be the father of kings

4. c. Duncan's eldest son

5. f. head was cut off and placed on a sword

6. g. King of Scotland

7. e. "Hover through the fog and filthy air"

8. d. executed for being a traitor

9. False

10. False

11. False

12. True

13. True

14. d. You must hide your true feelings

15. a. Duncan's guards

16. b. She wouldn't share her chestnuts.

17. c. She is furious.

18. b. He thinks they are women, but they have beards.

19. f. *Two truths are told, / As happy prologues to the swelling act of the imperial theme.*

20. c. *O worthiest cousin, / The sin of my ingratitude even now / Was heavy on me.*

21. d. *Come, you spirits / That tend on mortal thoughts, unsex me here, / And fill me from the crown to the topful / Of direst cruelty.*

22. b. *My noble partner / You greet with present grace and great prediction / Of noble having and of royal hope, / That he seems rapt withal. To me you speak not.*

23. a. *For brave Macbeth—well he deserves that name—/ Disdaining Fortune, with his brandished steel, / Which smoked with bloody execution, Like valor's minion carved out his bloody passage / Till he faced the slave*

24. e. *When the hurly-burly's done, / When the battle's lost and won.*

25. g. *I have spoke / With one that saw him die, who did report / That very frankly he confessed his treasons, / Implored your highness's pardon and set forth / A deep repentance.*

26. He fought bravely against Norway and Sweden, conquering many men, including Macdonwald.

27. Macbeth- Thane of Cawdor, King; Banquo-lesser than Macbeth, but greater; shall get (have) kings, but won't be one

28. She wants the spirits to take everything "womanly" away from her and make her just like a man so that she can have the courage and the strength to convince Macbeth without fear or remorse. She doesn't want to feel any emotions or have any "womanly" feelings.

Page 92: Act One Vocabulary Quiz

1. b. a cup or goblet

2. o. to punish by beating; criticize severely

3. d. deserving of shame; deeply wrong

4. n. to make or become gradually less until little remains

5. i. one that indicates or foreshadows what is to come; forerunner
6. a. 1) involved by logical necessity; entail, 2) appealed to; beseeched
7. g. lack of gratitude; ungratefulness
8. c. a period between two events
9. j. strength of character; determination
10. k. submissive follower or dependent
11. e. difficult or adverse situation
12. h. of, or a characteristic of, a prophet or prophecy
13. m. 1)to infer with little evidence; guess; 2) an idea or opinion based on little evidence; conjecture
14. l. things of little importance or value; small amounts
15. f. dried up or shriveled, as if from loss of moisture

Page 93: Act Two Quiz
1. i. has nightmares about the witches
2. c. Banquo's son
3. b. imagines a dagger leading him to the king's chamber
4. d. "Give me the daggers. The sleeping and the dead are but pictures."
5. a. "But this place is too cold for hell."
6. e. found the king dead
7. h. arrives with Macduff to wake the king
8. j. flees to England
9. f. sees the "daggers in men's smiles"
10. g. saw the king's horses eat each other
11. True
12. False
13. True
14. True
15. True
16. False
17. False
18. False
19. True
20. False
21. d. *Hear it not, Duncan, for it is a knell / That summons thee to heaven, or to hell.*
22. a. *A little water clears us of this deed. / How easy is it then!*
23. b. *By th' clock 'tis day, / And yet dark night strangles the travelling lamp.*
24. g. *Therefore to horse, / And let us not be dainty of leave-taking / But shift away.*
25. c. *He did command me to call timely on him; / I have almost slipped the hour.*
26. f. *The obscure bird / Clamored the livelong night. Some say the earth / Was feverous and did shake.*
27. e. *O come in, equivocator. Knock, knock, knock.*
28. The Porter comments on how like hell Macbeth's castle has gotten. The purpose is twofold: 1) He mentions some timely remarks to the "equivocator," which is in reference to the Gunpowder Plot. Also, the scene serves as comic relief, as the drunk Porter makes bawdy remarks about what drink does to men.
29. They are both guilty. They deal with the blood on their hands very differently. To Macbeth, the blood will never come clean—a statement that he will always feel guilty about what he's done—or so we assume. To Lady Macbeth, a "little water" cleans the blood off their hands easily. This indicates that Lady Macbeth can "wash her hands" of the entire incident and not be plagued with guilt—or so we are led to believe.
30. Lady Macbeth takes on the men's role and plants the daggers, therefore getting her hands bloodied in the act. The horses are seen eating each other, and the day is dark as night. (Others include a hawk being killed by a mousing owl, the horses broke out of their stalls against their men). Things are not right in the world. Evil is taking over, and what could have been considered the natural course of things has been altered.

Page 95: Act Two Vocabulary Quiz
1. h. loyalty to a ruler or country
2. l. to add something in order to make it larger or more substantial
3. e. drinking and becoming noisy
4. k. shouted and demanded noisily
5. a. a severe, serious, or desperate situation or circumstance
6. m. to cover with a substance; usually gold or gold-like
7. f. expressions of grief or sorrow
8. g. intention or desire to cause great harm to someone
9. b. able to be felt, touched
10. o. to talk or negotiate; speak with
11. c. appearing as most important, powerful; strongest or most common in number or amount
12. n. to stir emotion in someone; arouse
13. j. satisfied thirst or desire
14. i. moral or ethical considerations
15. d. calling for service or action

Page 96: Act Three Quiz
1. f. suspects Macbeth of murdering Duncan
2. e. safely escapes the ambush
3. a. "Be innocent of the knowledge, dearest chuck / Till thou applaud the deed."
4. c. "Naught's had, all's spent / Where our desire is got without content."
5. d. angry she was not consulted in Macbeth's affairs and to be able to show her "art"
6. g. refused Macbeth's summons
7. b. suspects Macbeth of Banquo's murder
8. h. safely living in England with King Edward
9. False
10. False
11. False
12. False
13. True
14. True
15. True
16. True
17. False

18. True
19. a. Macbeth; b. convincing the murderers to kill Banquo; c. he won't do the deed himself
20. a. Banquo; b. Banquo is suspicious of Macbeth; c. Macbeth senses this suspicion, so he has Banquo murdered.
21. a. Lady Macbeth; b. Macbeth sees Banquo's ghost at the feast and goes hysterical; c. Lady Macbeth must have an excuse for Macbeth's behavior, or some may become suspicious.
22. a. Lady Macbeth; b. Lady Macbeth is beginning to feel guilty about the way they rose to power; c. We start to see Lady Macbeth become weaker and feel bad about what they did, and we see Macbeth become the stronger one in the relationship.
23. Hecate is mad at the other witches, as she wanted to "play" by showing off what she could do to Macbeth. It may have been added as a break to the audience, since they have just witnessed Macbeth possibly slipping into insanity. It could also have been a scene so that the stagehands could disassemble any fancy staging or lighting that made Banquo's ghost appear.
24. Banquo expressed his suspicions before he was killed; Macduff does not show up for the feast; Lennox and the other Lord talk about their suspicions.
25. Before Duncan's murder, Macbeth thought about what he was about to do. He felt bad about murdering him. Before Banquo's murder, he was acting on impulse, trying to get him out of the way. He felt nothing about killing him, although he is then plagued by Banquo's ghost, which indicates his subconscious is getting to him. At first, Lady Macbeth "wore the pants" in the relationship. Lady Macbeth begins to weaken, and Macbeth falls deeper into his evil. Macbeth even then keeps Lady Macbeth in the dark about Banquo's murder and Macduff's family's murder, until Lady Macbeth slips into insanity.

Page 98: Act Three Vocabulary Quiz
1. a. a condition of great physical or mental distress
2. l. to put down; to tell someone off
3. g. secluded from the world
4. d. fearless; unable to be intimidated
5. h. unproductive or unsuccessful
6. n. wrestle or struggle with
7. e. made extremely angry
8. c. cheerful; happy
9. k. great evil or harm
10. f. religious; devout
11. m. removed something undesirable or imperfect
12. j. a ceremonial staff or rod
13. o. various; miscellaneous
14. b. a harsh or cruel leader
15. i. disgusting; wicked; unpleasant

Pages 99-100: Act Four Quiz
1. a. "beware Macduff"
2. b. "none of woman born shall harm Macbeth"

3. g. Macbeth cannot be harmed "until Great Birnam Wood to high Dunsinane hill / Shall come against him"
4. h. notifies Macbeth that Macduff has gone to England
5. j. wants to know if Banquo's descendants will reign.
6. d. entire family is slaughtered
7. e. delivers the bad news to Macduff
8. d. calls Macduff a traitor
9. c. a "prattler" beyond his years
10. i. tests Macduff to see where his allegiance lies
11. False
12. False
13. False
14. False
15. True
16. False
17. False
18. True
19. b. Macduff's son
20. a. Macbeth
21. c. Macduff
22. e. Lady Macduff
23. d. Malcolm
24. The row of eight kings that look like Banquo. He doesn't understand; it angers him because it confirmed the witches predictions and he is confused because he doesn't understand how the riddles of the other three apparitions will ever allow it to be.
25. It may be just a bit of comic relief before his family is killed. *Answers may vary.* It seems that Lady Macduff is bitter toward her husband and did not involve herself with his work.

Page 101: Act Four Vocabulary Quiz
1. g. intense sadness
2. l. internal organs, especially the intestines
3. e. praiseworthy; commendable
4. n. supreme authority or rule
5. a. has an extremely large number or amount; overflows
6. h. a childish act or gesture
7. c. having extreme desire for wealth; greedy
8. m. omens; foreshadowing
9. i. a physical or psychological disorder or disease
10. b. deadly or destructive
11. k. an animal or bird that is hunted
12. o. to enjoy or take pleasure in something
13. d. having, or motivated by, determination
14. j. a tank for storing water
15. f. without inhabitants; deserted

Pages 102-103: Act Five Quiz
1. b. wants the Doctor to give Lady Macbeth some medicine to "cure" her ills
2. a. "Out, damned spot! out, I say! – One, two. Why then, 'tis time to do 't. Hell is murky!"

3. f. "Tyrant, show thy face! / If thou be'est slain and with no stroke of mine, / My wife and children's ghosts will haunt me still."
4. d. Macbeth's servant
5. c. has heard Lady Macbeth confess to the murders
6. e. "Now does he feel his title/ Hang loose about him, like a giant's robe / Upon a dwarfish thief."
7. True
8. True
9. True
10. False
11. True
12. True
13. False
14. True
15. False
16. True
17. False
18. f. Young Siward
19. e. Macduff
20. a. Macbeth
21. d. Lady Macbeth's attendant
22. c. Seyton
23. b. Lady Macbeth
24. Malcolm orders the soldiers to carry branches from the woods of the Birnam forest and descend upon Dunsinane. Macduff was born via c-section and not vaginally, so he was considered "not born of woman."
25. Macbeth's soliloquy is all about the insignificance of us all and our time here on the earth. We are just players on the stage of life, taking our turn to speak our part, then exiting the stage to be heard no more. This is so depressing. I would like to think that as we grow up, we impact other people's lives enough that our memory goes on. I guess that's up to what we do with our own lives though. If you choose to just quickly "play" your part in life, rather than making the most of your time on the stage, then you can be easily forgotten. Life is what we make of it.

Page 104: Act Five Vocabulary Quiz
1. c. violent shaking or stirring; disturbance
2. e. to judge or settle a dispute
3. f. to consider a person guilty
4. i. connecting or relating to God or gods
5. j. makes stronger
6. n. uncontrollable anger or rage
7. o. people of good family or high social position
8. h. to damage or spoil
9. d. thick, gloomy, and hard to see through
10. a. something that disturbs or makes one anxious
11. b. annoyed constantly; bothered
12. l. remaining in a pure state; uncorrupted
13. k. move back suddenly
14. g. rebellions against authority
15. m. to criticize sharply; to reprimand

Page 105: Just for Fun! Crossword Puzzle

Pages 106-109: Macbeth Final Test
1. g. Donalbain
2. a. Macbeth
3. i. Porter
4. h. Hecate
5. k. Fleance
6. e. Duncan
7. n. Lady Macduff
8. f. Malcolm
9. d. Banquo
10. l. Lennox
11. m. the Three Witches
12. j. Ross
13. b. Lady Macbeth
14. o. Seyton
15. c. Macduff
16. d. You must hide your true feelings.
17. a. Duncan's guards
18. b. She wouldn't share her chestnuts.
19. b. Scotland and Norway
20. d. the Porter
21. d. "Thou shall get kings, though thou be none"
22. d. Siward
23. b. Inverness
24. b. Macduff
25. c. traitor
26. b. Malcolm
27. a. Macduff
28. c. a child holding a burning cross
29. a. He will be the father of kings
30. d. ambitious and motivated
31. Lady Macbeth
32. Malcolm
33. Lady Macbeth
34. Macduff
35. Lennox
36. Young Siward
37. Porter
38. Captain
39. Banquo

40. Young Macduff
41. Witches
42. Lady Macbeth
43. Banquo
44. Doctor
45. Attendant
46. Seyton

> *How did Macbeth earn the respect of the King in Act One?* Macbeth fought and defeated Macdonwald, cutting off his head and carrying it on his sword. He was a brave and valiant soldier who ended up practically single-handedly winning the war for Scotland.

> *Summarize the witches' prophecies for both Macbeth and Banquo.* Macbeth: Thane of Glamis (which he already was), Thane of Cawdor, and King; Banquo: Lesser than Macbeth, but greater, and that his children will be king although he will not be king.

> *Explain what Lady Macbeth asks the spirits to do to her to get her "ready" for the King's execution. Give as many details as possible.* Lady Macbeth receives Macbeth's letter—she vows to get rid of Duncan, but is afraid Macbeth is not man enough. She asks the gods to make her manly enough to take over if she has to. She asks the gods to replace her milk for gall.

> *Explain the content and purpose of the Porter and his speech in Act Two.* He is there for comic relief, now that the king has just been murdered. He proclaims that he is hell's gatekeeper. A farmer, a liar and a tailor all get to hell before the porter actually answers the door. He mumbles on about how alcohol affects a man—how it makes a man willing but unable to perform sexually. He also says that alcohol makes one's nose red, and makes one have to urinate more often.

> *Explain the significance of both Macbeth and Lady Macbeth getting blood on their hands in Act Two. How does each of them react to the blood? What does this reveal about their characters and their intentions?* Macbeth is overwhelmed with the amount of blood on his hands—a sign that he was not ready for and feels guilty for murdering Duncan. He says that all the water in the ocean will never make his hands clean. Lady Macbeth gets her hands bloody after she plants the daggers. She comes back to Macbeth, and easily washes her hands. She even comments that "a little water clears us of this deed." This makes us believe that she has no conscience about the murder.

> *Explain the meaning and significance of Macbeth's "Tomorrow" soliloquy (Act Five) in terms of the theme of the play and the universality of the message to you in your own life.* Macbeth's tomorrow speech is all about our time on this earth. We are all here for such little time on the earth, and the time we are here is insignificant. He is basically saying that life is nothing important, and that our brief time on this earth means nothing. He says this speech just

after he hears that his wife is dead, presumably by her own hand.

> *Explain the dramatic change in Macbeth since the beginning of the play. Be sure to include details about the differences in the murders of Duncan and Banquo, the appearance of the ghost, as well as his relationship with Lady Macbeth.* At the beginning of the play, Macbeth carries his guilt heavily. He does not want to murder Duncan, but is persuaded. He then has Banquo murdered very easily, although he does not do it himself. As he falls deeper into his paranoia and guilt, he sees Banquo's ghost appear at the feast, threatening him. He expresses his guilt and fears aloud as Lady Macbeth excuses his behavior. In the beginning of the play, he is considered a sissy by his wife's standards, and she easily manipulates him. Later, he kills Banquo without even consulting her. By the end of the play, she is weak and plagued by guilt and their roles have completely reversed.

> *Explain the dramatic change in Lady Macbeth from the beginning of the play. Be sure to include details about her motivations at the beginning of the play, her feelings towards Macbeth and the murders taking place and finally, her state of mind in Act Five.* In the beginning of the play, Macbeth is considered a sissy by his wife's standards, and she easily manipulates him. She is the evil one who masterminds the plan to kill Duncan, and after he is unable to complete the plan, she does it herself. Later, he kills Banquo without even consulting her. By the end of the play, she is weak and plagued by guilt and their roles have completely reversed. She is completely insane by Act Five, and demands a light by her at all times, possibly because she is afraid of the darkness inside and around her.

> *Explain the irony in Macbeth's line: "Infected be the air whereupon they [the witches] ride, / And damned all those who trust them!" from Act Four.* The ironic thing is that Macbeth himself trusted the witches from the very beginning. He was suspicious for about one minute, then decided that they knew everything and let them lead him. In the end, he is damned because he trusted the witches.

Pages 110-112: Macbeth Final Test
1. D. You mist hide your true your true feelings.
2. A. Duncan's guards
3. B. She wouldn't share her chestnuts.
4. B. Scotland and Norway
5. D. the Porter
6. D. "Thou shall get kings, though thou be none."
7. D. Siward
8. C. Inverness
9. B. Macduff
10. C. traitor
11. B. Malcolm
12. A. Macduff
13. C. a child holding a burning cross

14. A. He will be the father of kings
15. D. ambitious and motivated
16. D. Donalbain, Malcolm, and Macduff
17. D. Ross
18. D. he is making Malcolm the next king of Scotland
19. D. loyal and intuitive
20. B. convinced she wants Duncan dead
21. B. He blames them for killing the king.
22. C. 4
23. A. Scotland
24. C. the Porter
25. A. ambition
26. B. plants the bloody daggers
27. C. Macduff
28. B. run away
29. D. insists "life goes on"
30. A. washing her hands
31. A. Macbeth
32. C. Hecate
33. B. Banquo
34. B. Lady Macbeth
35. B. Macduff
36. A. Lady Macbeth
37. D. Malcolm
38. D. Lady Macduff
39. C. the Witches
40. C. Lady Macbeth